Table of contents

To the teacher

This student workbook will help reinforce the basic information presented in the textbook *Photo-Offset Fundamentals*. Each workbook unit is keyed to a specific chapter of the text. Questions of various types make up each unit. All the questions are objective, so it will be easy for the student or teacher to check the answers. The questions in this workbook have been designed to supplement the review questions in the textbook.

There are several different ways in which to use this workbook.

- The students could be asked to answer the questions as homework after a chapter has been discussed in class.
- The units of the workbook could be assigned for periods of supervised study in the classroom.
- A teacher may use a unit of the guide as an objective quiz to check students' mastery of material in the text.
- Each student may be allowed to complete the units at his or her own rate.

In addition to the objective questions, this guide contains the following:

- A student information sheet that may aid the teacher in designing projects to meet the needs of individual students
- A table on which students can record their scores for each unit
- A form on which students can record shop regulations
- A safety pledge for students to sign
- An accident report form

Photo-Offset Fundamentals
Student Workbook

by
John E. Cogoli

Keyed to the textbook
Photo-Offset Fundamentals, 5th Edition
by John E. Cogoli

Bennett & McKnight
a division of
Glencoe Publishing Company

Glencoe Publishing Company
17337 Ventura Boulevard
Encino, CA 91316

10 9 8 7 6 5 4 3 2 1

ISBN 0-02-675600-5

Printed in the United States of America

To the student

Answering the questions in this workbook will help you learn the material in *Photo-Offset Fundamentals*. Each unit in this workbook has the same number as the textbook chapter it reviews. Often, several units are devoted to reviewing a single chapter. These units carry the number of the chapter they review. They are lettered in alphabetical sequence—for example, Unit 1A, Unit 1B, Unit 1C.

The questions in each unit will help you recognize and remember the important facts found in the textbook. Answering the questions will also help you see how well you understand the material you have read.

To begin working with this workbook, do the following:

1. Fill out the Student Information Form on page **17.** This sheet will help your teacher become better acquainted with you.

2. In the form on page **11** list the safety regulations that your teacher gives you. You will be expected to follow those regulations in the classroom and in the shop.

3. Read the safety pledge following the list of regulations. Sign the pledge to show that you will follow the safety rules.

4. Complete the units of this workbook as your teacher assigns them.

5. Keep a record of your scores on the chart on page **15.**

Several different types of questions are used in this workbook. Samples of each type are shown below. Study the samples so that you will know the correct way to answer each question.

Completion: Study the sentence and decide what word, or words, would correctly complete the thought. Write the missing word in the blank at the left.

Alaska   1. SAMPLE: The largest state in the United States is _____.

blue   2. SAMPLE: The three primary colors are red, yellow, and _____.

True or False: Read the statement carefully and decide whether it is true or false. Write T in the space if the statement is correct and F if it is false.

T   3. SAMPLE: Washington, DC, is the capital of the United States. (T or F)

Multiple Choice: Read the question and the possible answers. Write the letter of the correct answer in the answer blank.

New York   4. SAMPLE: A state that is east of the Mississippi River is _____.
   a. Colorado
   b. Arizona
   c. New York
   d. North Dakota

Matching: Match each item in the left-hand column to an item in the right-hand column. Write the letter of the correct choice in the answer blank at the left.

SAMPLE: Place the letter of each description on the right next to the game it best describes.

	Games	**Descriptions**
b	5. Baseball	a. A game in which players try to throw a round ball through a hoop
a	6. Basketball	b. A game played with a hard ball and bat
c	7. Football	c. A game in which teams score touchdowns and field goals

SAMPLE: In the blank next to each country, place the letter of the continent on which that country is located. Some letters may be used more than once.

	Countries	**Continents**
c	8. United States	a. Asia
a	9. India	b. Europe
a	10. China	c. North America
b	11. Portugal	
c	12. Canada	

SAMPLE: Place the letter of each geometric figure next to its correct name.

c	13. Square
a	14. Triangle
b	15. Circle

Identification: An identification question is usually accompanied by an illustration. Identify each lettered part of the illustration by writing the correct letter in the answer blank to the left, next to the term it correctly identifies.

SAMPLE: In the blanks at the left, identify by letter each part of the illustration shown in Figure A.

a	16. Chimney
d	17. Roof
b	18. Door
c	19. Window
e	20. Wall

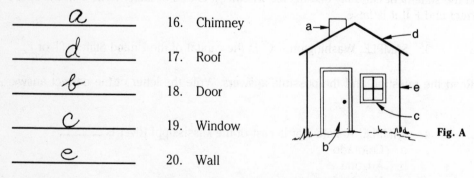

Fig. A

8

Correct Sequence: The textbook assignment will describe the order of a procedure. The question will list these steps, out of sequence. In the blanks at the left, you are to letter the steps so that they will be in the correct order from top to bottom.

SAMPLE: The main steps in making and soldering a wire splice are listed below. Letter the steps (a through e) in the sequence in which they should be performed.

_____*e*_____ 21. Solder the splice.

_____*d*_____ 22. Apply soldering flux.

_____*a*_____ 23. Remove the insulation.

_____*b*_____ 24. Scrape the bare wires.

_____*c*_____ 25. Splice the wires.

Shop and safety regulations

1. _____

2. _____

3. _____

4. _____

5. _____

6. _____

7. _____

8. _____

9. _____

10. _____

Safety pledge

I pledge that I will follow all of the safety rules discussed in *Photo-Offset Fundamentals.* I will also follow all of the safety regulations given by the instructor. I will not use a press, machine, papercutter, camera, or exposure device without permission of the instructor. I will report all accidents to the instructor immediately, no matter how small they are. I will help to maintain a safe shop by working at my own business and by not bothering other students.

Date _____   Name _____

Student guide scores

Unit	Possible Score	Number Correct	Unit	Possible Score	Number Correct
1	29		12B	23	
2	20		13A	24	
3	33		13B	21	
4A	39		14	25	
4B	32		15A	29	
4C	21		15B	41	
5A	27		16A	40	
5B	30		16B	26	
5C	27		16C	36	
5D	36		16D	42	
5E	50		16E	26	
6	34		17A	46	
7A	31		17B	32	
7B	24		18A	48	
8A	31		18B	22	
8B	31		18C	38	
9A	49		19	25	
9B	45		20	21	
10A	40		21	25	
10B	41		22	28	
11	49		23	22	
12A	23				

Student information

1. Name _____
                Last   First   Middle

2. Home address _____

3. Home phone number _____

4. Class _____

5. School attended last year _____

6. Homeroom _____

7. Father's name _____

8. Father's occupation _____

9. Father's work phone number _____

10. Mother's name _____

11. Mother's occupation _____

12. Mother's work phone number _____

13. Hobbies and outside interests _____

    _____

14. Previous shop experience _____

    _____

15. Name of family doctor _____

16. Doctor's address _____

17. Doctor's phone number _____

Accident report

1. Name of injured _____

   Address _____

   Telephone _____

   Homeroom _____

2. Date of injury _____

3. Nature of injury (cut, burn, foreign matter in eye, etc.) _____

   _____

4. Tools or machines involved _____

5. Witnesses to accident: Name _____

   Address _____

   Name _____

   Address _____

6. Treatment: First aid _____ By whom? _____

   Physician _____ Address _____

   Hospital _____ Address _____

7. Cause of accident (Explain fully.) _____

   _____

   _____

8. Correction (What will be done to prevent similar accidents?) _____

   _____

   _____

   Report filed by _____

   Date _____

Unit 1
INTRODUCTION TO PHOTO-OFFSET PRINTING

(pages 1–12)   PHOTO-OFFSET FUNDAMENTALS

_____ 1. Photo-offset lithography is one of the applied _____ arts.

_____ 2. On the offset plate, the image is level with the _____ area of the plate.

_____ 3. Offset printing is made possible by a basic chemical fact: _____ and water do not readily mix.

_____ 4. The surface of an offset plate is treated to hold a thin film of _____.

_____ 5. The two kinds of areas on a prepared offset plate are the _____ areas and the clear areas.

_____ 6. The _____ areas of the offset plate surface are composed of greasy, fatty ink.

_____ 7. The _____ areas of the plate have no ink.

Refer to Figure 1-A. Identify the various parts of the offset printing system by entering the correct letters in the blanks at the left.

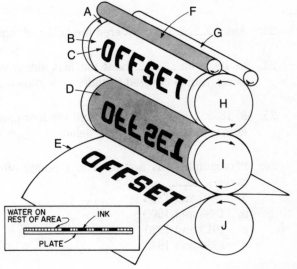

Fig. 1-A

_____ 8. Impression cylinder

_____ 9. Ink form roller

_____ 10. Blanket

_____ 11. Blanket cylinder

_____ 12. Offset plate

_____ 13. Printed sheet

_____ 14. Clear area of plate

_____ 15. Water form roller (dampener)

_____ 16. Image on plate

_____ 17. Plate cylinder

_____ 18. Moisture (water, fountain solution) will stick only to the _____ area of the plate.

_____ 19. Applied ink will stick only to the _____ areas of the plate.

Identify the type of image (readable or wrong-reading) that appears at different locations on the offset printing press.

	Location	**Type of image**
_____ 20.	Blanket	a. Readable
_____ 21.	Plate	b. Wrong-reading
_____ 22.	Printed sheet	

_____ 23. Alois _____ is considered the father of lithography.

_____ 24. In 1903, Ira _____ built the first lithographic press that included an offset, rubber-covered cylinder now known as a blanket cylinder.

_____ 25. In 1839, Louis _____ invented the first practical process for producing lasting photographs in fine detail.

_____ 26. Photography was first used to produce offset plates in the period between _____.
   a. 1880 and 1890
   b. 1890 and 1900
   c. 1910 and 1920
   d. 1930 and 1940

_____ 27. In the _____ process printing method, a rubber-blade squeegee forces ink through a stencil.

_____ 28. In the plate _____ process, the image may be outlined with a graver, and then etched with acid.

_____ 29. The two printing processes described in Unit 1 that print directly onto the paper from a raised inked surface are flexography and _____.

Unit 2
CAREERS IN OFFSET PRINTING

(pages 13–23)   PHOTO-OFFSET FUNDAMENTALS

_____ 1. A person called a _____ plans and directs the company operation.

_____ 2. A person who writes copy for advertising is called a _____.

_____ 3. A printing company's art department might also be called the design or _____ department.

_____ 4. The design of a printed piece is the work of the _____ designer.

_____ 5. A lithographic artist is also called a dot etcher or a _____.

_____ 6. A person who sets type is called a _____.

_____ 7. A person who reads the typeset copy for errors is called a _____.

_____ 8. Type and illustrations are arranged and assembled according to layout by a _____ artist.

_____ 9. Process camera operators make _____ of the copy in the desired size.

_____ 10. The offset stripper is also called the film _____.

_____ 11. The _____ receives the flats and makes the actual printing plates for the press.

_____ 12. The person who readies the offset press and runs off the required number of press copies is called a press _____.

Refer to Figure 2-A. Answer the following questions.

_____ 13. The film negative was produced by the _____ operator.

_____ 14. The type for the text and the headlines were set by the _____.

_____ 15. The _____ artist arranged and assembled all typeset materials and illustrations on the layout sheet before the layout was photographed.

_____ 16. The negatives were mounted on a masking sheet, called a _____, by a stripper.

_____ 17. The stripped-up negatives, mounted on the masking sheet, are then sent to the _____ who uses the flat to produce an offset plate.

Fig. 2-A

_____ 18. The cutting, folding, perforating, and stitching of finished printed sheets are done by _____ workers.

_____ 19. When a school, a bank, or other establishment has its own printing plant, that facility is often called an _____ printing department.

_____ 20. Quick printing shops are often small, with minimal equipment, dealing primarily with walk-in trade. (T or F)

Unit 3
SAFETY

(pages 25–30)   PHOTO-OFFSET FUNDAMENTALS

_____ 1. You should never work alone in the lab. (T or F)

_____ 2. Only severe injuries need to be reported to the instructor. (T or F)

_____ 3. The permission of the _____ is necessary before you may mix any solutions.

_____ 4. Do not operate or adjust any equipment unless your _____ has given you permission.

_____ 5. When mixing solutions, keep the solutions at _____ length.

_____ 6. When mixing or pouring chemicals, wear safety glasses or a face _____ over your prescription glasses.

_____ 7. Smoking is never allowed in the lab or darkroom. (T or F)

_____ 8. When pouring a liquid from a large container into a smaller container, place the smaller container in a _____.

_____ 9. The correct order for mixing a solution of chemicals and water is to _____.

    a. pour the water into the chemicals
    b. pour the chemicals into the water
    c. pour either into the other

_____ 10. Wear _____ gloves when your hands must contact irritants that might cause skin infections.

_____ 11. A rubber _____ will keep chemicals from staining your clothing and reaching your skin.

_____ 12. Unless an _____ fan is operating in the darkroom, don't mix or weigh chemicals there.

_____ 13. Gasoline, benzene, toluene, turpentine, carbon tetrachloride, and kerosene should never be used in the shop. (T or F)

_____ 14. When solvents are being used, the shop should be adequately ventilated to remove the solvent that has _____.

_____ 15. Used rags are placed in an _____, self-closing container.

_____   16. For safety's sake, before using machinery you should remove obstructive clothing and jewelry. (T or F)

_____   17. Never operate a machine above the maximum speed specified by the _____.

_____   18. A helper should do only those jobs assigned by the approved _____ of the press.

_____   19. When operating the press, the _____ guard should always be in place.

_____   20. Never lubricate or wash a press unless the press is _____.
      a. stopped
      b. running
      c. inching
      d. in reverse

_____   21. Avoid using the stripping _____ as a workbench.

_____   22. When cutting film, keep your fingers back from the guiding edge of the straight edge or _____.

_____   23. Do not attempt to remove the glass top of the stripping _____.

_____   24. Keep your fingers out of the rollers of the folding _____.

_____   25. The card cutter, or the film cutter, is a one-person device. (T or F)

_____   26. The papercutter should be operated by only one person at a time. (T or F)

_____   27. If another person is using the papercutter, you are not allowed within _____ of the machine.

_____   28. You are not allowed to remove or install a cutter blade (knife) unless your _____ gives you specific permission to do so.

_____   29. You should never try to operate the papercutter controls with one hand. (T or F)

_____   30. If operating a hand-lever papercutter, keep both hands on the lever until the lever reaches the extreme up position on the upstroke. (T or F)

_____   31. To avoid burns, exposure lights in cameras and platemakers should be allowed to _____ before you change or handle them.

_____   32. When possible, push on a wrench rather than pulling on it. (T or F)

_____   33. When you must hammer, grind, or chip metal, wear _____ to protect your eyes.

Unit 4A
JOB PLANNING AND LAYOUT

(pages 31–37)   PHOTO-OFFSET FUNDAMENTALS

_____   1. In planning a printing job, the only decisions involve type, page proportions, and format. The purpose of the printed piece and its intended audience do not need to be considered. (T or F)

Refer to Figure 4-A. Complete the following sentences, which describe parts of the printed typeface image.

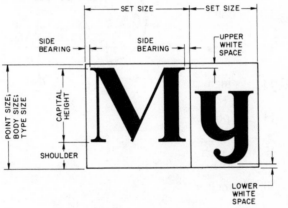

Fig. 4-A

_____   2. Metal type sizes are determined by the height in points of the entire _____ of the type.

_____   3. The _____ space beneath the character allows for the descender strokes of the lowercase letters such as *p* and *y*.

_____   4. The point size of a printed character includes the upper white space, the _____ height, and the shoulder.

Refer to Figure 4-B. Complete the following sentences.

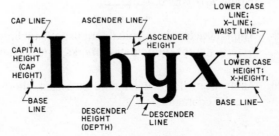

Fig. 4-B

_____ 5. Cap height is measured vertically from base line to the _____ line.

_____ 6. The ascender height is measured vertically from the x-line to the _____ line.

_____ 7. Another name for x-height is _____ height.

_____ 8. The x-height is measured vertically from cap line to x-line. (T or F)

Refer to Figure 4-C. Place the letter of each indicated line gauge measurement in the blank next to its correct reading.

_____ 9. ½ inch

_____ 10. 6 picas

_____ 11. 6 points

_____ 12. 9 picas

_____ 13. ⅞ inch

Fig. 4-C

_____ 14. 72 points

_____ 15. 1⅛ inch

_____ 16. ¼ inch

_____ 17. 36 points

_____ 18. 18 points

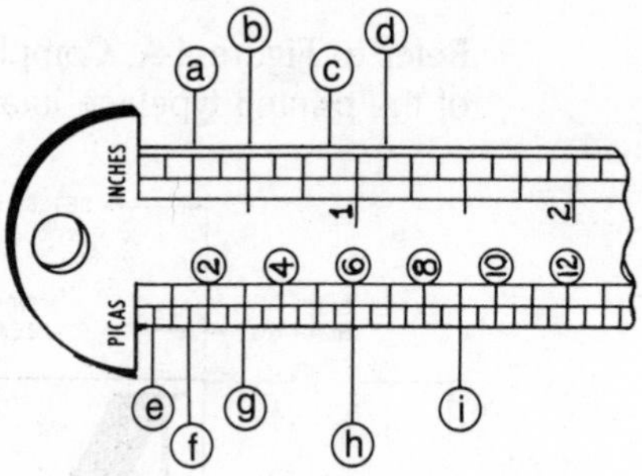

_____ 19. The width of a 10-point em equals _____ points.

_____ 20. In advertising, a two-column ad, 1 inch deep, would be priced at _____ agate lines.

_____ 21. Ems and ens are frequently referred to as _____ quads and en quads.

_____ 22. An agate formerly denoted _____ point type.

_____ 23. On a printed page, artwork or a block of typeset copy is referred to as an _____.

_____ 24. A complete set of all the type images of a certain size in a particular typeface is called a _____.

_____ 25. The characters in a typical font usually include _____ letters, lowercase letters, figures, punctuation marks, and sometimes accented letters.

_____ 26. Aside from the usual letters of a font, there are special letters called _____ characters.

_____ 27. A group of variations of one typeface is called a type _____.

_____ 28. A book set in all caps of a text type (like Old English) would be easy to read. (T or F).

_____ 29. Slanted type is usually called _____ type.

_____ 30. Several sizes of the same typeface are called a type _____.

_____ 31. Type sizes are measured in _____.

_____ 32. Type in sizes _____ points and larger is generally referred to as display type.

_____ 33. Type that is 12 points and smaller is referred to as text or _____ type.

_____ 34. Some phototypesetting machines use sizing _____ to produce type in the size required.

_____ 35. Leading is the extra space between _____ of type.

_____ 36. Lines of type that are set without leading are said to be set _____.

_____ 37. Line spacing is measured from base line to _____ line of two consecutive lines of type.

_____ 38. Line spacing includes the _____ size of the type plus the leading between the two lines.

_____ 39. Line spacing is also referred to as _____ advance, line feed, or line advance.

Unit 4B

JOB PLANNING AND LAYOUT

(pages 36–41)   PHOTO-OFFSET FUNDAMENTALS

_____ 1. Format refers to the overall _____ and form of the printed work.

_____ 2. A proportion of _____ to 6 is a popular and pleasing proportion for a printed page.

Refer to Figure 4-D. Identify by letter each of the major components of a pair of facing book pages.

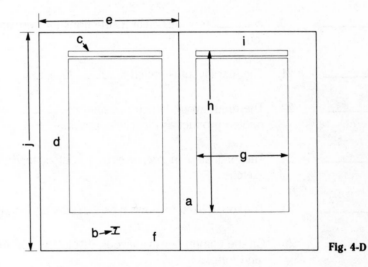

Fig. 4-D

_____ 3. Page number

_____ 4. Running head

_____ 5. Outside margin

_____ 6. Width of single page

_____ 7. Gutter

_____ 8. Foot

_____ 9. Depth (height) of text

_____ 10. Width of text

_____ 11. Head

_____ 12. Height of page

Match the composition format with the kind of composition that best describes it.

	Composition Format	**Kind of Composition**
_____	13. Unjustified left and right	a. Justified
_____	14. Only the first line overhangs the body	b. Ragged right
_____	15. Only the first line is indented	c. Ragged right and left
_____	16. Flush left and right	d. Hanging indention
_____	17. Unjustified on left, justified on right	e. Square indention
_____	18. Flush left, unjustified on right	f. 1-em indention
_____	19. No indention	g. Ragged left

_____ 20. A _____ provides clear instructions for everyone who is to work on that job.

_____ 21. The first layout is called a _____ layout.

_____ 22. The final layout, which is called the _____ layout, resembles the final printed product as closely as possible.

_____ 23. The first step in preparing a layout is to draw several small _____ sketches.

_____ 24. The rough sketch shows type _____ and locations.

_____ 25. On the comprehensive layout, display type is shown in its actual _____ and form.

_____ 26. Display type may be traced from type _____ sheets or type tracing cards.

_____ 27. On the comprehensive layout, text type is usually indicated by drawing a _____ or square.

_____ 28. The layout artist keys the manuscript copy to its _____ on the comprehensive layout.

Using the proportions of 4 to 6, as shown in Figure 4-E, calulate the desired dimension for each of the following:

———————————————   29. Height of a 5-inch-wide card

———————————————   30. Width of a 12-inch-high page

———————————————   31. Width of a 9-inch-high page

———————————————   32. Height of a 7-inch-wide page

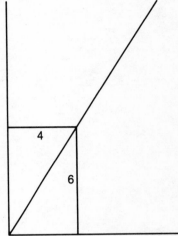

Fig. 4-E

Unit 4C

JOB PLANNING AND LAYOUT

(pages 42–44)　　　　　　　　PHOTO-OFFSET FUNDAMENTALS

1. The procedure of determining how much space the manuscript copy will take up in the final printed product is called _____.

The four basic steps in copyfitting are listed below. In the blanks on the left, letter these operations (a, b, c, and d) in the sequence in which they should be carried out.

2. Determine the total number of lines to be printed.

3. Determine the total number of pages required.

4. Determine the total number of characters in the manuscript.

5. Determine the amount of space required to print the total number of lines.

6. A _____-pitch machine types all characters the same width.

7. Most of the printers used with microcomputers have a _____ pitch.

8. In counting the number of characters in 1 inch of manuscript line, do not count spaces. (T or F)

9. Six lines of manuscript, each 5 inches in length, have a total of 300 characters. How many characters are there per inch of manuscript copy?

10. Five lines of manuscript copy measure 5, 5½, 5½, 6, and 5 inches, respectively. What is the average line length in inches?

11. Suppose there are 10 characters per inch in a manuscript line of 7 inches. How many characters are there in the line?

12. A manuscript has 340 lines of 40 characters each. What is the total number of characters?

13. Assume that a chosen typeface of a 9-point size has an average of 3.04 type characters per pica. How many type characters are there in 890 lines of 25-pica measure?

14. A manuscript has a total of 50,175 characters. There will be 45 printed characters in a line. How many lines will there be?

15. Typing line-for-line means that the typist will type each page so that the page will have the number of characters desired in the _____ page.

_____ 16. In typing line-for-line, set the typewriter carriage for the number of _____ to be contained in a typeset line.

_____ 17. A type specimen sheet for display type shows the exact width of each _____.

_____ 18. In most cases, illustration copy must be enlarged or reduced to fit properly in the printed product. (T or F)

_____ 19. In a dummy, display type and illustrations should be indicated in their actual size and position. (T or F)

_____ 20. A running _____ is often a chapter title appearing at the top of the page.

_____ 21. Trim lines indicate the size the page will be after the head, foot, and outside edge have been _____.

Unit 5A

METHODS OF TYPE IMAGE COMPOSITION
FOR REPRODUCTION

(pages 46–50)   PHOTO-OFFSET FUNDAMENTALS

_____ 1. In its broadest sense, composition means the production and arrangement of all _____ to be printed.

_____ 2. In common usage, composition usually refers to the production of _____.

_____ 3. Composition of type is now called setting type or _____ type.

_____ 4. The worker who composes type is called a typesetter or _____.

_____ 5. The first proofs of type composition are called _____ proofs.

_____ 6. Slicks, repros, and etch proofs are other names for reproduction _____.

_____ 7. Whatever the method of setting type, the final result is a visible type image on paper, film, or an offset plate. (T or F)

_____ 8. Typesetting methods can be broadly classified as either hot type or _____ type composition.

_____ 9. In hot type composition, type is cast from molten _____.

_____ 10. In hot type composition, galleys are _____ that are made (pulled) on a proof press.

Place the letter of each description in the blank to the left, next to the type method it best describes.

Type Method   **Description**

_____ 11. Monotype®   a. Casts each line of type as a solid slug

_____ 12. Linotype® and Intertype®   b. Individual type characters cast in whole lines according to copy

_____ 13. Foundry type

                                        c. Individual type characters set by hand

_____ 14. Cold type composition is also called _____-dimensional type.

_____ 15. Cold type involves the production of images on paper or on _____.

_____   16. Hand lettering is especially useful for display lines in larger sizes. (T or F)

_____   17. Mechanical composition is one kind of hot type composition. (T or F)

_____   18. A T-square and triangle should be kept clean by washing them occasionally with _____ and water.

_____   19. Guidelines may be drawn with a _____ pencil.

_____   20. One method of correcting an error in mechanical cold type composition is to paint over the error with China _____.

_____   21. A ballpoint pen produces an inked line that is more uniform in width than a technical pen. (T or F)

_____   22. Used with a T-square and triangles, the technical pen can be used for ruling business _____.

_____   23. The technical pen can be used for underscoring typeset composition. (T or F)

_____   24. Callouts and leaders can be drawn on a transparent film overlay that is taped in _____ to (over) the original artwork.

_____   25. Lettering on an overlay avoids damage to the original artwork. (T or F)

_____   26. The technical pen may be inserted into a special _____ for drawing circles and arcs.

_____   27. When used for drawing, the technical pen should be held _____.
a. vertically against the guide edge
b. slanted to the left of the guide edge
c. slanted to the right of the guide edge

Unit 5B
METHODS OF TYPE IMAGE COMPOSITION
FOR REPRODUCTION

(pages 50–59)   PHOTO-OFFSET FUNDAMENTALS

Place the letter of each description in the blank next to the item it best describes.

Item   **Description**

_____ 1. Ruling pen   a. Paste-up-ready illustrations

_____ 2. Template   b. Letters in sheet form

_____ 3. Clip art   c. For drawing inked lines

_____ 4. Preprinted type   d. For tracing lettering

_____ 5. The purchase of clip art gives you the right to reproduce it. (T or F)

_____ 6. In using adhesive type, the _____ on the letters and on the layouts help you to align the letters.

_____ 7. An error in dry-transfer lettering may be picked off the artwork with a piece of _____ tape or white paper adhesive tape.

_____ 8. Sample copies of existing, already printed work can be used as camera _____.

_____ 9. A _____ of a printed halftone may result in its losing its dot structure.

_____ 10. A photostat is right-reading. (T or F)

_____ 11. The word *stat* is short for _____.

_____ 12. Stats are photocopies on _____ paper.

_____ 13. Photomechanical transfer is a _____ transfer process.

_____ 14. Typewriter-style composition is called cold type composition. (T or F)

_____ 15. When a typewriter-style machine uses type bars to strike an impression, it is called _____ (or strike-on) composition.

_____ 16. A typewriter-style machine that uses a laser to produce its images is said to produce nonimpact composition. (T or F)

_____ 17. On many standard typewriters, the typed characters and the spaces between words are of equal _____.

_____ 18. The number of characters per inch produced by a typewriter is known as the _____.

_____ 19. When counting typed characters, include the spaces, symbols, and _____ marks.

_____ 20. A _____-spacing typewriter provides a choice of spacing between words.

_____ 21. In the justified style of composition, the lines are flush left and _____ right.

_____ 22. Depending on the capability of your typewriter, you can justify the typed copy either manually or _____.

_____ 23. Manual justification of typed copy usually requires that the copy be typed _____ times.

_____ 24. The simplest method of reproducing typewritten copy in the offset process is to type directly onto a paper master called a _____-image offset plate.

_____ 25. On the personal computer, the keyboarded copy is stored on a _____.

_____ 26. The device that changes computer signals so that they can be sent over a phone line is known as a _____.

The four basic steps in the operation of the laser printer are listed below. In the blanks at the left, letter these steps in the order in which they take place.

_____ 27. The drum attracts toner.

_____ 28. The laser beam traces characters onto a light-sensitive drum.

_____ 29. Toner is applied to the paper.

_____ 30. On the paper, the toner forms the characters outlined by the laser.

Unit 5C
METHODS OF TYPE IMAGE COMPOSITION
FOR REPRODUCTION

(pages 59–62)   PHOTO-OFFSET FUNDAMENTALS

Place the letter of each description in the blank next to the generation it best describes.

Generation	Description
1. First generation	a. CRT phototypesetter
2. Second generation	b. Laser phototypesetter
3. Third generation	c. Electro-photomechanical in design
4. Fourth generation	d. Adaptation of hot-metal typecasting machine

_____   5. In phototypesetting, the controlled projection of _____ produces two-dimensional images of type characters.

_____   6. Phototype 12 points or larger in size is called _____ type.

_____   7. Phototype less than 12 points in size is called _____ type.

Refer to Figure 5-A, which shows a simplified phototypesetting system. Place the letter of each part in the blank next to its correct name.

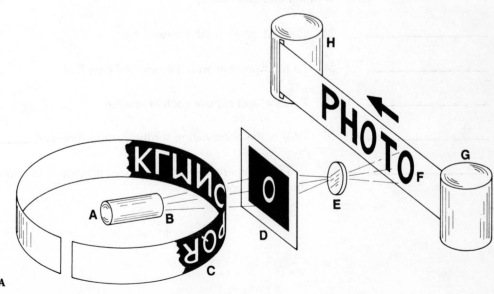

Fig. 5-A

_____ 8. Exposure-limiting gate

_____ 9. Phototype on phototypesetting paper

_____ 10. Exposure light

_____ 11. Supply cassette

_____ 12. Light beam

_____ 13. Sizing lens

_____ 14. Type font

_____ 15. Receiving cassette

_____ 16. On film or photo paper, a _____ image is one that is not yet visible—it needs to be developed.

_____ 17. At the end of the typesetting job (at the end of the *take*), processing makes the type images _____ and permanent.

_____ 18. RC refers to _____-coated phototypesetting paper.

_____ 19. The abbreviation for stabilization paper is _____.

_____ 20. Stabilization paper has a _____ incorporated into its emulsion.

_____ 21. Some photodisplay typesetters also set phototype in _____ sizes.

_____ 22. By means of a _____ in the phototypesetting machine, you can produce phototype in a wide range of sizes.

The three main steps in the operation of the manually operated photodisplay typesetter are listed below. Letter these operations (a, b, or c) in the sequence in which they take place.

_____ 23. Cut and develop the exposed type.

_____ 24. Fit the typesetter with the selected type font.

_____ 25. Position and expose each character.

_____ 26. CAM is the abbreviation for the composition and _____ terminal.

_____ 27. In a newspaper shop, full newspage makeup is commonly performed by the _____ operator.

Unit 5D
METHODS OF TYPE IMAGE COMPOSITION FOR REPRODUCTION

(pages 62–66)   PHOTO-OFFSET FUNDAMENTALS

_____ 1. Automated phototypesetters set entire galleys of fully _____ and justified text type.

_____ 2. A direct-entry phototypesetter is designed to be operated primarily from its _____.

_____ 3. Output speed of the direct-entry phototypesetter is primarily limited by the speed of the _____.

The units of a typical direct-entry phototypesetter include

_____ 4. A standard typewriter-style _____

_____ 5. An electronic photodisplay _____ (screen)

_____ 6. A memory _____ (buffer)

_____ 7. A mini_____

_____ 8. A phototype-character-_____ optical system

_____ 9. The mirror is part of the typesetting machine's _____ system.

_____ 10. The mirror in the escapement system is programmed to position each character horizontally along the line of _____.

_____ 11. Linespacing means to advance the phototypesetting paper horizontally. (T or F)

Identify the movement (a or b) needed to perform each of the operations listed below.

Operation   **Movement**

_____ 12. Hyphenation   a. Vertical advance

_____ 13. Line spacing   b. Horizontal positioning

_____ 14. Justification

_____ 15. Film advance

_____ 16. Leading

_____   17. Successive type characters

_____   18. Spacing between lines

_____   19. Paper advance

_____   20. The procedure of preparing the phototypesetter to produce phototype in the desired face, size, and format is known as _____.

_____   21. The manual entering of copy through the keyboard of the phototypesetter or other keyboard-equipped machine is known as _____.

The basic steps in the operation of a keyboard-operated phototypesetter are listed below. Letter these operations (a through f) in the sequence in which they are usually performed.

_____   22. Characters enter the minicomputer and buffer memory.

_____   23. Operator keyboards the characters.

_____   24. Operator manually keyboards the hyphenation.

_____   25. The machine signals when a line reaches the justification zone.

_____   26. Operator signals for a return.

_____   27. Operator begins to keyboard the next line.

_____   28. A separate-entry phototypesetter is also called a _____ typesetter, or an off-line typesetter.

Refer to Figure 5-B. Identify by letter each of the components of a typical separate-entry phototypesetter.

_____   29. Lenses

_____   30. Prism

_____   31. Type font disk

_____   32. Signal or tape reader

_____   33. Memory storage (buffer)

_____   34. H & J computer

_____   35. Exposure light source

_____   36. Phototype

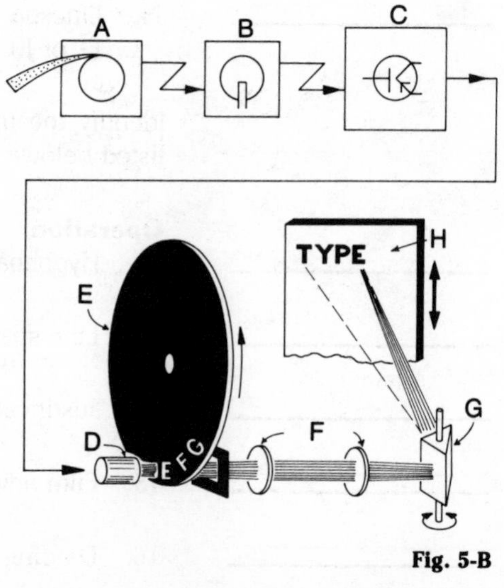

Fig. 5-B

44

Unit 5E
METHODS OF TYPE IMAGE COMPOSITION
FOR REPRODUCTION

(pages 65–75)   PHOTO-OFFSET FUNDAMENTALS

Refer to Figure 5-C. Place the letter of each component in the blank next to its correct name.

_____   1.   OCR typewriter

_____   2.   Line printer

_____   3.   News service (wire line)

_____   4.   Phototype

_____   5.   Video typewriter

_____   6.   OCR reader

_____   7.   Systems controller

_____   8.   Video typewriter

_____   9.   Video display layout terminal (VDL) or composition and makeup terminal (CAM)

_____   10.   Hard copy

_____   11.   Phototypesetter

_____   12.   Video display editing terminal (VDT)

_____   13.   Processor

_____   14.   An editor can use a VDT to recall a story from the controller _____.

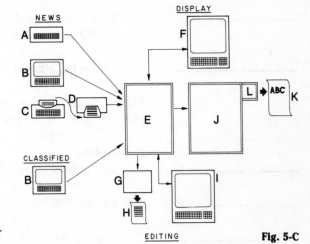

Fig. 5-C

Place the letter of each description in the blank next to the unit of the electronic page makeup system that it best describes.

Unit	Description
15. Control unit	a. Resembles a television screen
16. Keyboard	b. Contains disk drive and memory

_____ (for 15)

_____ (for 16)

_____ 17. Monitor   c. For typing the text

_____ 18. Graphics tablet   d. For designing the style of the page

_____ 19. Software   e. Produces the type

_____ 20. Laser printer   f. Instructions for driving the computer

_____ 21. In automatic hyphenation, a _____ is built into the computer.

_____ 22. In a digitized typesetting system, each type character has been converted to a pattern of _____.

_____ 23. Each digitized dot is numbered and identified by its location in the horizontal and _____ rows.

_____ 24. CRT is the abbreviation for _____ ray tube.

Each of the descriptions below refers to one of the systems listed on the right. Place the letter of the system in the answer blank next to its description.

Description   **System**

_____ 25. Glass photo negative   a. Dot-mosaic (digitized)

_____ 26. Pattern of dots   b. Raster line

_____ 27. Digitally encoded

_____ 28. Scan line pattern

Refer to Figure 5-D. Place the letter of each component of the CRT raster-line phototypesetting system in the blank next to its correct name.

_____ 29. Font grid

_____ 30. Copy memory storage

_____ 31. Condenser lens

_____ 32. Pickup photo cell

_____ 33. Tape or signal reader

_____ 34. H & J computer

_____ 35. Printout CRT

_____ 36. CRT beam-deflection circuitry

_____ 37. Sizing lens

_____ 38. Objective lens

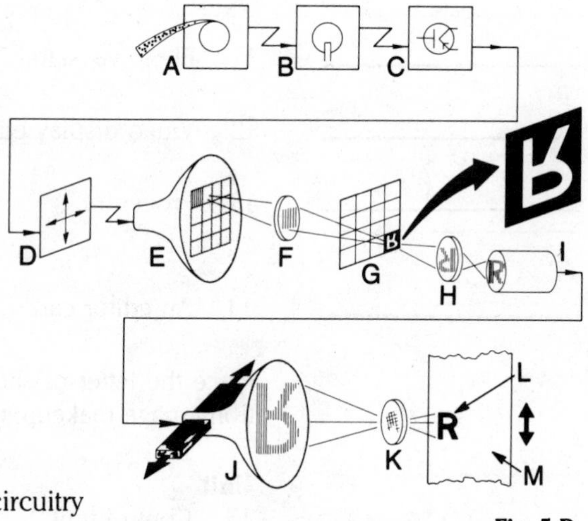

Fig. 5-D

_____   39. Phototype

_____   40. Phototype paper or film

_____   41. Character selection CRT

Refer to Figure 5-E. In the blanks, identify each of the lettered components in the diagram of the third generation dot-mosaic style phototypesetter.

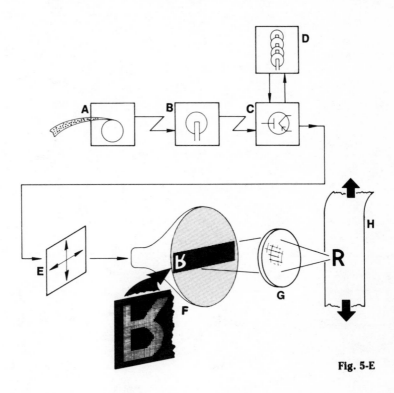

Fig. 5-E

_____   42. H & J computer

_____   43. Signal or tape reader

_____   44. Sizing lens

_____   45. Magnetic disk font storage

_____   46. CRT dot-deflection circuitry

_____   47. Printout CRT

_____   48. Phototype on film or paper

_____   49. Laser is an acronym for light amplification by stimulated emission of _____.

_____   50. A phototypesetting system that transmits characters that are generated directly onto the offset plate is called a direct computer-to-_____ system.

Unit 6
PROOFREADING

(pages 78–82)   PHOTO-OFFSET FUNDAMENTALS

_____   1. Proofreading is the process of reading proofs of type composition to find _____.

_____   2. Proofs are read by _____.

_____   3. A second proof, made after errors have been corrected, is called a _____ proof.

In the blanks, insert the proper proofreader's marginal symbol for each of the following corrections:

_____   4. Wrong front

_____   5. Insert space

_____   6. Delete

_____   7. Let it stand

_____   8. Period

_____   9. Comma

_____ 10. Begin a paragraph

_____ 11. No paragraph

_____ 12. Question mark

_____ 13. Apostrophe

_____ 14. Less space between words

_____ 15. Defective letter

_____ 16. Lowercase letter

_____ 17. Set in Roman type

_____ 18. Set in boldface type

_____ 19. Set in lightface type

Refer to Figure 6-A, which shows six steps in the correction of a typographical error on a VDT. These steps are listed below. In the blanks at the left, letter them (a through f) in the sequence in which they should take place.

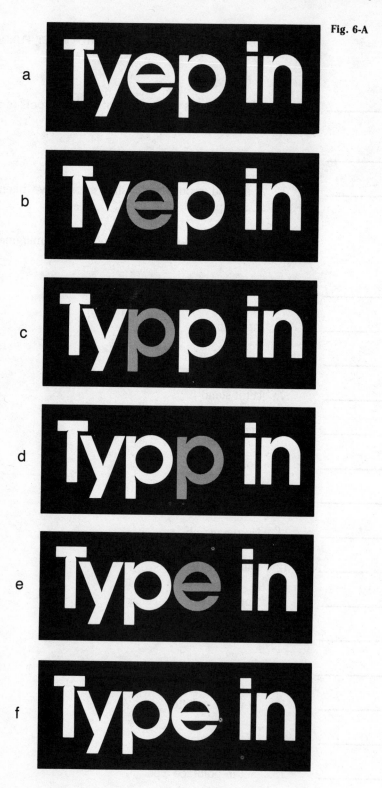

Fig. 6-A

a

b

c

d

e

f

_____   20.   Cursor positioned over wrong letter *e*.

_____   21.   Correct letter *e* is keyboarded.

Unit 7A

PREPARING COPY FOR THE CAMERA

(pages 83–89)   PHOTO-OFFSET FUNDAMENTALS

_____   1. Items that will be copied (photographed) by the camera are called _____ copy.

_____   2. The film negatives that result from photographing the camera copy will be used to make offset _____.

_____   3. The _____ layout, a board with its attached copy, is also called a page paste-up, paste-up, or mechanical.

_____   4. Another name for the paste-up artist is the _____.

_____   5. Three kinds of copy are line, _____, and color.

_____   6. Usually, only one piece of copy is mounted on each paste-up. (T or F)

_____   7. Line copy is copy that has _____.
         a. two tones
         b. gradations of tone
         c. only one tone
         d. three tones

_____   8. The density throughout line copy is _____.
         a. varied
         b. proportional
         c. uniform
         d. uneven

_____   9. Original line drawings are generally drawn at _____ times the final desired reproduction size.

_____   10. A screened halftone print—a photo that has already been printed as a screened halftone—is classified as _____ copy.

_____   11. Halftone copy is copy that has gradations or variations in _____.

_____   12. Halftone copy is also called continuous-_____ copy.

Classify the examples below as line copy or halftone copy by entering _a_ or _b_ in the answer blank.

Example	**Classification**
13. Pen-and-ink line drawing	a. Line copy
14. Proof of phototype	b. Halftone copy

_____   15. Original photograph

_____   16. Original oil painting

_____   17. Eliminating parts of an illustration to focus attention on one part of it is known as _____.

_____   18. You can make your crop marks on a tissue _____ taped over the original photography.

_____   19. A printed halftone on which line copy appears is known as a _____ print.

_____   20. Overprinting and _____ are other names for a combination print.

_____   21. A combination halftone print is said to have _____ printing when type is shown in white letters on the halftone.

_____   22. The best way to prepare a combination print is to attach the _____ copy to an acetate overlay that is registered to the photoprint in exact position.

_____   23. Copy is always reproduced same size as the original. (T or F)

_____   24. Line drawings are usually drawn larger and then reduced to minimize imperfections. (T or F)

_____   25. On the process camera, several pieces of copy that will be reproduced at different sizes will be photographed on separate pieces of _____.

Refer to the table below. Using a proportional calculator, calculate the missing dimension or reproduction percentage. (All measurements are in inches.)

	Original Height	Original Width	New Height	New Width	Reproduction Percentage of Original
26.	4	10	3	7½	?
27.	5½	8¼	5	7½	?
28.	5	10	7	14	?
29.	6¼	9	8	?	128%
30.	4½	6	3	?	67%
31.	7	14	?	8	57%

Unit 7B

PREPARING COPY FOR THE CAMERA

(pages 89–96)   PHOTO-OFFSET FUNDAMENTALS

_____ 1. A screen tint may be introduced by placing a commercial screen tint between the _____ and the plate during the plate exposure.

_____ 2. A screen tint area may also be produced by _____ the plate.

_____ 3. In double-burning, one exposure is made on the plate through the screen tint; a second exposure is made through the _____ for the job.

_____ 4. Screen tints have a wide number of screen tint _____.

Indicate the screen tint usually used for the purposes listed below.

Purposes   **Screen Tint**

_____ 5. Newspapers   a. 110 or 120 lines per inch

_____ 6. Rough papers or easier press runs   b. 133 lines per inch

_____ 7. Commercial offset printing   c. 150 lines per inch

_____ 8. Smooth coated paper   d. 65 or 85 lines per inch

_____ 9. During the plate exposure, the emulsion side of the screen tint is toward the plate. (T or F)

_____ 10. A portion of a selected pattern of adhesive type shading sheet may be pasted down on the desired area of the original _____.

_____ 11. A device called a halftone screen _____ can be used to determine the ruling count of a printed halftone illustration.

_____ 12. The halftone screen _____ to be used is indicated to the camera operator on the tissue overlay of the illustration.

_____ 13. The closer the lines of the halftone screen used (on the proper paper), the finer the detail in the printed picture. (T or F)

_____ 14. A _____ paste-up is a paste-up of a number of pages for the printing of one full side of a press sheet.

_____ 15. All pieces of copy for a paste-up should have equal density of _____.

_____ 16. Light blue guidelines will not reproduce when _____.

17. When you paste up the copy, align the three lines on the copy with the lines on the _____.

18. A _____ scale can be used to find the center of an illustration or type proof.

19. Marking the center of a line of type can be done conveniently through the zero center _____ of the centering scale.

20. An _____ is a second, third, or fourth sheet attached over the original, in register, on the paste-up board.

21. The marks used to align the paste-up sheet and the overlays are called _____ marks.

22. Ruled lines can be produced by setting the lines along with the _____ during the typesetting procedure.

23. Ruled lines can be produced by scribing them on the _____.

24. Ruled lines can be drawn with pen and ink on the _____ proof.

Unit 8A
LINE PHOTOGRAPHY

(pages 97–105)   PHOTO-OFFSET FUNDAMENTALS

_____   1. The general term for the procedures involved in photographing copy is
                       _____ photography.

_____   2. Line copy generally consists of copy that is printed in _____ ink on
                       white paper.

Refer to Figure 8-A. Identify by letter the basic parts of the horizontal process camera listed below.

Fig. 8-A

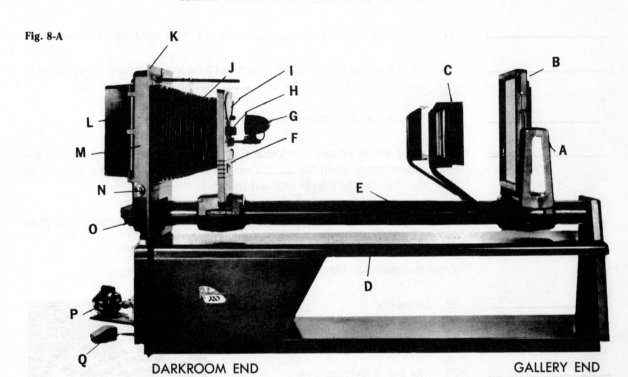

DARKROOM END   GALLERY END

_____   3. Lamps

_____   4. Iris control

_____   5. Copyboard carriage

_____   6. Bellows

_____   7. Copyboard

_____   8. Front case

_____   9. Flashing lamp

_____   10. Foot switch

_____   11. Lens

_____   12. Vacuum film holder

_____   13. Vacuum pump and motor

_____   14. Rear case

_____   15. Darkroom controls

_____   16. The _____ is composed of several separate optical glass elements assembled into a barrel.

_____   17. A slip-fit protective lens _____ is provided for the front of the lens.

_____   18. The diaphragm (iris) blades open or close to form a circular opening to adjust the correct amount of _____ admitted through the lens.

_____   19. The abbreviation for focal length of the lens is _____.

_____   20. Focal length equals one-fourth the distance from the copyboard to the ground glass when the _____ on the ground glass is the same size as the copy on the copyboard and in focus.

_____   21. Each f/stop number expresses the _____ of the diaphragm opening as a fraction of the focal length of the lens.

Refer to Figure 8-B. Identify the parts of the diaphragm control.

_____   22. Index line

_____   23. (Cursor) pointer

_____   24. The f/stop division scale

_____   25. The f/stop percentage bands

_____   26. Proper setting of the diaphragm control automatically adjusts the _____ for the proper f/number.

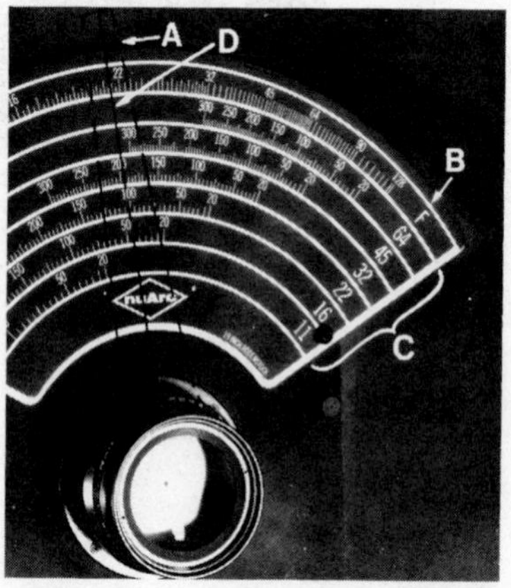

Fig. 8-B

Place the letter *a* or *b* in the blank next to the statement that best describes it.

	Description	**Side of Film**
_____	27. Contains the image	a. Base side
_____	28. Light-sensitive coated	b. Emulsion side
_____	29. Clear side when processed	
_____	30. Anti-halation side	

_____ 31. On a typical processed line negative made with lith-type film the image is clear transparent and the background appears solid _____.

Unit 8B
LINE PHOTOGRAPHY

(pages 105–118)   PHOTO-OFFSET FUNDAMENTALS

Refer to Figure 8-C, which shows the basic setup for line photography. Identify each of the parts.

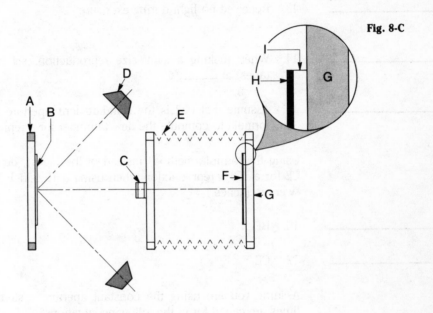

Fig. 8-C

_____   1.   Film base

_____   2.   Bellows

_____   3.   Film holder

_____   4.   Light

_____   5.   Film emulsion

_____   6.   Copyboard

_____   7.   Lens

_____   8.   Copy

_____   9.   Film

Place the letter *a* or *b* (designating one of the developed negative film areas) next to the statement that best describes the area.

Description	Developed Negative Film Area
10. Nonimage area	a. Black areas
11. Image area	b. Clear (transparent) areas
12. Struck (affected) by light	
13. Received no light during exposure	

_____

_____

_____

_____

_____   14. When making a same-size reproduction, set both BE and CE (both tapes) at _____%.

_____   15. Assume that f/22 is the standard lens aperture for same size. Use the formula to compute the new f/number for a reproduction of 30%.

Using the formula method (instead of the tapes), determine the BE and the CE for a 150% reproduction when using a 10½-inch FL lens. (Give your answers in inches.)

_____   16. BE

_____   17. CE

Assume you are using the constant aperture system. What new exposure times are called for in the following situations?

_____   18. A 95% reproduction; basic exposure of 20 seconds

_____   19. A 55% reproduction; basic exposure of 30 seconds

_____   20. A 200% reproduction; basic exposure of 10 seconds

_____   21. An _____ lens is useful when a piece of copy is to be reduced or enlarged in only the height or width.

_____   22. Suppose you have a basic exposure of 20 seconds and you wish to use a filter that has a factor of 2. What is the new length of exposure?

The basic steps in line photography are listed below. By lettering them (a through i), designate the order in which the operations take place.

_____   23. Check focus and size.

_____   24. Evaluate the negative.

_____   25. Set lensboard and copyboard for reproduction percentage.

_____   26. Make the exposure.

_____   27. Place copy in copyboard.

_____   28. Set timer for exposure.

_____   29. Set diaphragm control for reproduction percentage.

_____   30. Place film on vacuum back.

_____   31. Process the film.

Unit 9A
HALFTONE PHOTOGRAPHY

(pages 119–131)   PHOTO-OFFSET FUNDAMENTALS

_____ 1. Copy that contains gradations of tone is known as _____ copy.

_____ 2. Other names for halftone copy include _____-tone copy, C.T. copy, and contone copy.

_____ 3. A printed halftone illustration has dots and squares of varying sizes. (T or F)

_____ 4. Before photographing halftone copy, a halftone _____ is placed over the film in the camera.

_____ 5. The halftone dot pattern creates an optical _____. It is not actually a continuous-tone picture.

Refer to Figure 9-A. Identify each of the numbered areas in the three-part illustration as a *highlight, midtone,* or *shadow* area.

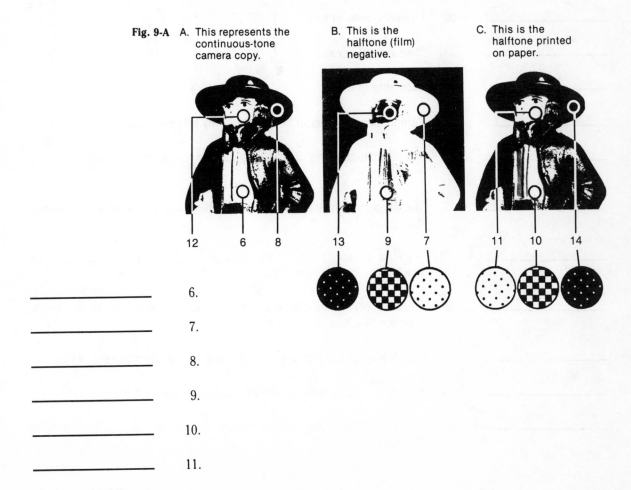

Fig. 9-A A. This represents the continuous-tone camera copy.

B. This is the halftone (film) negative.

C. This is the halftone printed on paper.

_____ 6.

_____ 7.

_____ 8.

_____ 9.

_____ 10.

_____ 11.

_____   12.

_____   13.

_____   14.

_____   15. Autoscreen® film has a screen pattern built into its _____ during manufacture.

_____   16. Contact screens are used in direct contact with the _____ in the camera.

Refer to Figure 9-B. Identify each part of the basic setup for halftone photography.

Fig. 9-B

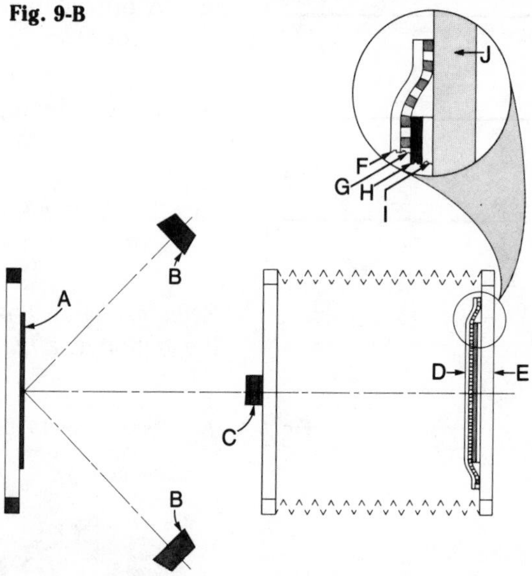

_____   17. Light

_____   18. Lens

_____   19. Vacuum film holder

_____   20. Emulsion side of screen

_____   21. Copy

_____   22. Emulsion side of film

_____   23. Base side of screen

_____   24. Base side of film

_____   25. Contact screens should be handled only by their _____.

_____   26. When photographing _____ original copy, gray contact screens are always used.

_____   27. The magenta contact screen has vignetted _____ of a magenta-colored dye.

_____   28. Magenta contact screens are used for making halftone _____ from black-and-white camera copy.

_____   29. A contact screen should be about a(n) _____ larger in width and height than the film it is to be used with.

_____   30. The degree of blackness in a film negative is known as optical _____.

_____   31. The term _____ refers to the measuring of optical density.

_____   32. Opacity is the ability of a material to prevent _____ from passing through it.

The basic steps in the three-part method of making a single-color halftone negative are listed below. In the blanks to the left, list the steps (a through h) to indicate the sequence in which they are usually performed.

Steps

_____ 28. Make the camera setup.

_____ 29. Remove the screen and film.

_____ 30. Calculate the exposures.

_____ 31. Make the bump exposure.

_____ 32. Store the screen.

_____ 33. Make the flash exposure.

_____ 34. Process the film.

_____ 35. Make the main exposure.

In evaluating a halftone negative, remember the following points:

_____ 36. The dots should be _____, not brown.

_____ 37. The shadow dots should range from _____% to about 25% to 30% black.

_____ 38. The highlight areas should have a dot of about _____%.

_____ 39. Midtones should range from about a _____% dot to a 70% dot.

_____ 40. A _____ exposure that is too long tends to close up the dark areas.

_____ 41. The _____ process is used to make halftone negatives from already printed halftones.

_____ 42. Rescreening means to photograph a halftone print through a _____.

_____ 43. Autoscreen® film has a dot pattern built into the film's _____.

_____ 44. Producing duotones requires the making of _____ halftone negatives.

_____ 45. The second color of a duotone is usually printed at a screen angle of _____ degrees to the first color.

Unit 10A
COLOR REPRODUCTION

(pages 149–158)   PHOTO-OFFSET FUNDAMENTALS

_____ 1. The two main classes of color printing are flat color printing and _____ color printing.

_____ 2. A prism spreads a beam of sunlight into a visible _____.

_____ 3. One millimicron equals one millionth of a _____.

_____ 4. White light is a combination of all colors of the _____.

_____ 5. In an additive color mixture, light rays of certain colors are _____ to other light rays to produce a new color.

List the color that is produced by mixing light of the following colors:

_____ 6. Blue light + red light + green light

_____ 7. Red light + green light

_____ 8. Green light + blue light

_____ 9. Blue light + red light

_____ 10. On the color wheel, _____ colors are opposite colors.

What color is seen by the eye when the following colors of ink are combined?

_____ 11. Cyan ink and yellow ink

_____ 12. Cyan ink and magenta ink

_____ 13. Magenta ink and yellow ink

_____ 14. Yellow ink, magenta ink, and cyan ink

In each of the following three series, select the color of filter usually used as one of the three filters in process-color-separation photography:

_____ 15. Black, blue, white, yellow

_____ 16. Purple, orange, green, brown

_____ 17. Red, white, amber, purple

_____ 18. A blue filter transmits blue light and absorbs _____ and red light.

_____ 19. The color that is the absence of all color sensation is _____.

_____ 20. In process-color-separation photography, a colored original is separated into the _____ colors.

Identify the following examples as reflection copy or transparent copy:

Examples   **Kinds of Copy**

_____ 21. An oil painting (on canvas) of a woodland scene   a. Reflection copy

                                                                            b. Transparent copy

_____ 22. A 35-mm slide of a person's portrait on color film

_____ 23. A color photo of a house on photoprint paper

_____ 24. A 16-mm movie film frame of animals

_____ 25. A water color painting (on paper) of flowers

_____ 26. For transparent copy, the camera lights are placed behind the camera _____.

_____ 27. To make the separation negatives for process-color-separation reproduction, _____ film is used.

_____ 28. The color-control patches show a record of the _____ densities.

_____ 29. The _____ scale is used to measure and compare density and density range on the separation negatives.

Listed below are the basic steps in the making of each color separation negative in the direct method of color separation. In the blanks at the left, letter these steps (a through j) in the correct order to indicate the sequence in which they are performed.

Steps

_____ 30. Make the flash exposure.

_____ 31. Install proper safelight in darkroom.

_____ 32. Mount copy on copyboard.

_____ 33. Make camera and lens settings.

_____ 34. Place film on vacuum back.

_____ 35. Set timer for exposure.

_____ 28. Color correction is done on contone film positive.

_____ 29. Color-corrected halftone negative is made by contact printing.

_____ 30. Reproduction is printed.

_____ 31. A set of _____ proofs generally includes one for each of the three process colors and one for black.

_____ 32. Four-color presses apply all four inks (wet) in one run. (T or F)

_____ 33. In flat color printing, the minimum number of colors given by the use of red ink on a yellow sheet is _____.

_____ 34. Mechanical masking may be used when type matter on a single flat is to appear in different colors on the same printed sheet. (T or F)

_____ 35. Ruby masking film is a commercially available peelable film affixed (in manufacture) to a _____-film base.

_____ 36. A separate clear acetate sheet, carrying type matter, that is placed over the layout sheet in register is called a(n) _____ sheet.

_____ 37. Linework that has areas of separate flat colors can be photographed to produce one negative for each color by photographing through _____.

_____ 38. The principal color in a duotone is generally printed at an angle of _____ degrees.

_____ 39. The second color in a duotone is made at an angle that is _____ degrees from the first color.

_____ 40. Original copy for a duotone is generally a black-and-white photograph. (T or F)

_____ 41. Fake color is another method of _____ separation.

Unit 11
FILM DEVELOPING AND DARKROOM PROCEDURES

(pages 169–188)   PHOTO-OFFSET FUNDAMENTALS

_____ 1. The light that is generally placed over the darkroom sink so you can inspect the negatives is called a _____.

_____ 2. What should be the height, in inches, of the safelight wall switches?

_____ 3. Wall switches for the darkroom general lighting should be at least _____ feet from the floor.

_____ 4. The purpose in developing exposed film is to make its _____ image visible.

The four trays used in the conventional developing of film are listed below. Letter these (a through d) in the order in which they are usually arranged from left to right in the darkroom.

_____ 5. Fixer

_____ 6. Running water

_____ 7. Developer

_____ 8. Shortstop

_____ 9. The _____ bath causes the latent image to become visible.

_____ 10. The _____ bath removes unexposed silver and the anti-halation backing.

_____ 11. The running _____ removes any traces of remaining chemicals from the film.

_____ 12. The _____ bath neutralizes the action of the developer.

_____ 13. You should avoid using the type of acetic acid called _____.

_____ 14. Fixer is also commonly called _____.

_____ 15. The sensitivity-guide method of developing film uses a _____ scale (sensitivity guide) to control development.

_____ 16. The still-development method of tray development is not effective for developing negatives of dot-for-dot copy. (T or F)

_____ 17. The tray-agitation method of processing film causes fresh developer to wash across the _____ areas of the film.

_____ 18. A contact print is a same-size reproduction on film or on _____.

_____ 19. A pinpoint contact-printing light source minimizes image _____.

_____ 20. A _____ scale can be used as a test negative to determine correct degree of contact-printing exposure.

_____ 21. On a contact photoprint made from a film _____, the image area appears black, and the background appears white.

_____ 22. In making a positive photoprint (on paper) from a film negative, the film negative is placed _____ side down over the paper.

Refer to Figure 11-A. Match the image shown there with the statement below. Enter either an *a* or a *b* in the answer blank.

Fig. 11-A

Idle Fox a

Idle Fox b

_____ 23. Looks like a film positive

_____ 24. Contact printed from a film negative

_____ 25. Looks like a film negative

_____ 26. Contact printed from a film positive

_____ 27. Could be called a reverse photoprint

_____ 28. Could be called a positive photoprint

_____ 29. Halftone contact prints are sometimes called _____ prints because of the trade name of the photopaper used.

_____ 30. You can make contact prints on photopaper from either a film _____ or a film positive.

_____ 31. A diazo film contains no _____ in its emulsion.

_____ 32. Lateral reversal means to flop an _____ from left to right, or vice versa.

_____ 33. In a negative–positive _____ print, half the image is black and half is white.

Indicate whether each of the descriptions applies to a spread or a choke.

Descriptions   **Technique**
_____ 34. Makes type look bolder   a. Spread

_____ 35. Makes type look thinner   b. Choke

_____ 36. Creates an overlap

_____ 37. Contacted on film from a negative

_____ 38. Contacted on film from a film positive

_____ 39. You can contact-print a halftone film negative from a contone film positive by placing a contact _____ between the two films in the printing frame.

Refer to Figure 11-B, which illustrates the technique of surprinting. Identify each of the lettered elements.

Fig. 11-B

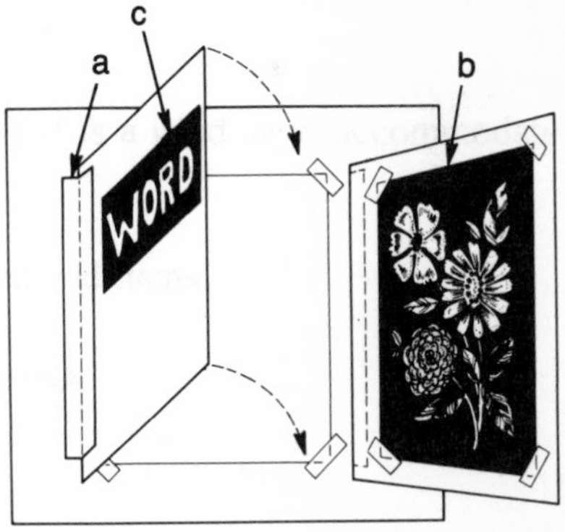

_____ 40. Halftone negative

_____ 41. Line negative

_____ 42. Hinge

                 43. _____ pins are the most accurate method of registering multiple exposures.

_____ 44. To make a contact-printed screened-type effect on photopaper, a patterned _____ is inserted between the film negative and the print paper in the contact frame before exposure.

_____ 45. In making a photoprinted enlargement on paper, the _____ is placed emulsion side up on the enlarger easel (base or bed).

_____ 46. In making a photoprinted enlargement on paper, the film _____ is placed emulsion side down in the negative carrier.

_____ 47. To make an enlarged halftone screened photoprint on paper from a contone negative, place the C.T. negative in the negative carrier with its

_____   12. Leading edge of the press sheet

_____   13. Distance from the leading edge of the plate to the leading edge of the press sheet

_____   14. On a film negative, the image usually appears wrong-reading when viewed from the _____ side.

_____   15. All pinholes and other "show through" defects on a negative are to be coated with _____.

_____   16. Scribing reference lines into the _____ of the negatives will help you place the negatives accurately on the layout.

_____   17. When taping negatives to the flat, never tape the negatives any closer to the image than _____.

_____   18. In taping negatives to the flat, match the three reference lines on the _____ with the corresponding reference lines on the rectangle on the flat.

_____   19. One way to crop a halftone negative on the flat is to use strips of masking _____ on all four sides.

_____   20. The expression "four up" means that a sheet (job) will be cut into _____ identical pieces after printing.

_____   21. Creep is noticeable when a saddle-stitched booklet is trimmed and the inside pages are progressively _____ than the outer pages.

_____   22. Three common methods for registering complementary flats are by cutouts, by register marks on film, and by the use of register _____.

_____   23. An example of step-and-repeat work is exposing one image several times on one _____.

Unit 12B
LAYING OUT AND STRIPPING THE FLAT

(pages 200–212)   PHOTO-OFFSET FUNDAMENTALS

1. A positive flat is usually composed of film _____.

2. The stock material for a positive flat is a sheet of transparent _____.

Refer to Figure 12-B, which shows a flat that is stripped positive. Identify the lettered items.

Fig. 12-B

3. Master layout

4. Image position

5. Light table surface

6. Centerline

7. Transparent flat

8. Transparent tape

9. Film positive

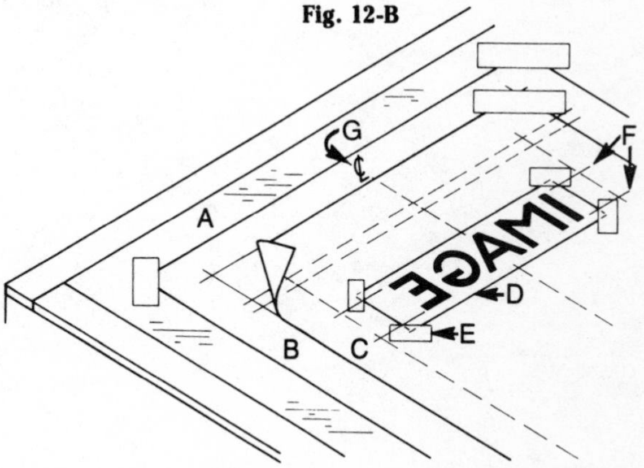

10. The four process-color-separation negatives are the yellow, the _____, the cyan, and the black.

11. Each of the four separation negatives will be stripped up on a separate _____.

12. The use of plastic sheets for the flats avoids misregister that might be caused by changes in _____.

13. _____ pin holes are punched in the four flats to be stripped up.

14. The color-separation negative that is first placed in registration on its flat over the base flat has the color of _____.

15. On the separation flats, all negatives are stripped with the emulsion side up. (T or F)

16. In process-color-separation stripping, the base-flat exposure mask is made of a sheet of clear _____.

17. The separation-negative-flat mask allows the plate exposure light to pass through only the stripped-up _____ negative.

_____ 18. When opened flat, the pagination dummy will indicate the _____ of the pages for the front and back of that sheet.

_____ 19. In printing "one up" in one color, the number of impressions required for each sheet is _____.

_____ 20. A layout that will result in two or more duplicate images in one impression is known as a _____-and-repeat layout.

_____ 21. In work-and-tumble, the number of plates used for the front and back of the sheet is _____.

_____ 22. The number of plates used for work-and-turn printing in one color is _____.

_____ 23. For sheetwise printing in one color, the number of plates used for a backed-up sheet is _____.

88

Unit 13A
PLATEMAKING

(pages 213–220)   PHOTO-OFFSET FUNDAMENTALS

_____ 1. The two separate areas on an offset plate are the clear area and the _____ area.

_____ 2. In manufacture, the surface of the plate is grained so it will be receptive to _____.

_____ 3. The term *master* is another name for the word _____.

_____ 4. Most metal plates are made of _____.

Refer to Figure 13-A. Identify each of the styles of plate ends.

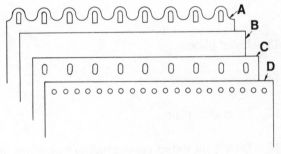

Fig. 13-A

_____ 5. Straight cut

_____ 6. Slotted (oval hole)

_____ 7. Serrated (looped)

_____ 8. Punched (round hole or pin-bar punched)

_____ 9. A plate is gummed to protect its _____ area from dirt and oxidation.

_____ 10. If a plate is to be stored, the gum coating acts as a _____.

_____ 11. A gum solution of _____ degrees Baumé is recommended for gumming a plate on the bench.

_____ 12. If you intend to store a plate for a considerable length of time, apply a coating of _____ gum.

Refer to Figure 13-B. Identify each of the lettered items.

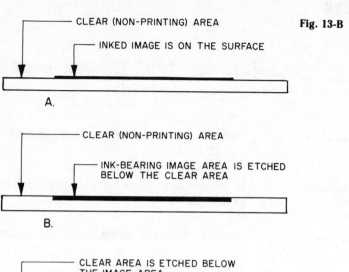

CLEAR (NON-PRINTING) AREA

Fig. 13-B

INKED IMAGE IS ON THE SURFACE

A.

CLEAR (NON-PRINTING) AREA

INK-BEARING IMAGE AREA IS ETCHED BELOW THE CLEAR AREA

B.

CLEAR AREA IS ETCHED BELOW THE IMAGE AREA

INK-BEARING IMAGE AREA

C.

_____ 13. Relief plate

_____ 14. Surface-coated plate

_____ 15. Deep-etch plate

_____ 16. During the offset-press printing operation, the dry-offset plate requires only inking—it requires no _____.

Refer to Figure 13-C. Identify the lettered items.

_____ 17. Flat

_____ 18. Negative with readable image

_____ 19. Tape

_____ 20. Plate

_____ 21. Gray scale (in cutout)

_____ 22. A vacuum _____ ensures the closest contact between the flat and the plate.

_____ 23. The gray _____ acts as a "measuring stick" for proper and consistent plate exposure.

_____ 24. When one image is repeated a number of times on a single light-sensitive plate, the plate-exposure method is called step-and-_____ work.

Fig. 13-C

Unit 13B
PLATEMAKING

(pages 220–232)   PHOTO-OFFSET FUNDAMENTALS

_____ 1. A typewriter can be used to place an image on a _____-image plate.

_____ 2. A negative-working plate is used with flats made up of film _____.

_____ 3. When developed, a negative-working plate yields a positive image. (T or F)

_____ 4. When developed, a positive-working plate yields a positive image. (T or F)

_____ 5. A positive-working plate is used with flats usually made up of film _____.

_____ 6. If a regular film negative is stripped into a flat for a positive-working plate, that finished plate will show the negative's image as a reverse image. (T or F)

_____ 7. During the developing of an additive type of plate coating, the image is intensified by adding a _____ to the printing area only.

_____ 8. On plates with a subtractive coating, the lacquer coating is applied at the factory over the entire _____ surface.

The steps in the preparation of a negative-working presensitized plate are listed below. Letter these steps (a through d) in the order in which they are performed.

Steps

_____ 9. Desensitize the plate

_____ 10. Expose the plate behind a flat composed of negatives

_____ 11. Develop (lacquer) the plate

_____ 12. Gum the plate

_____ 13. Wipe-on plates are sensitized in the shop, as needed, by coating them with a _____ sensitizer.

_____ 14. You can make a small repair (addition) to a broken image on a gummed metal plate by scratching through the gum just deep enough to make the plate ink-receptive, and then rubbing printing _____ into the scratch.

Refer to Figure 13-D, which shows a laser facsimile system. Identify the lettered parts.

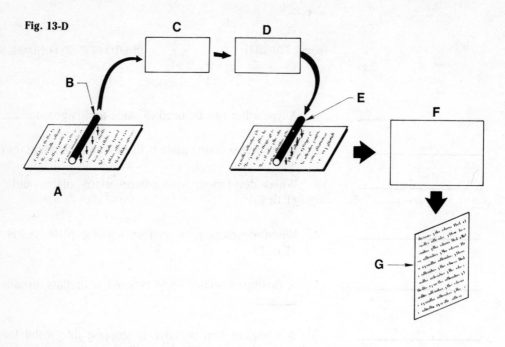

Fig. 13-D

_____ 15. Sensor

_____ 16. Modulator

_____ 17. Press-ready plate

_____ 18. Exposure laser

_____ 19. Reading laser

_____ 20. Automatic plate processor

_____ 21. Paste-up reading station

Unit 14
OFFSET INKS

(pages 233–238)   PHOTO-OFFSET FUNDAMENTALS

_____ 1. On the press, ink emulsification could cause _____ (ink tinting) on the clear areas of the printed sheets.

_____ 2. Most offset inks consist of a _____, pigments, and modifiers.

_____ 3. The ingredient that gives ink its color is the _____.

_____ 4. Inks of various colors that are kept on hand by the ink manufacturers are referred to as _____ colors.

_____ 5. In mixing inks for color, you generally add the _____ colors to the weaker colors.

_____ 6. Adding small amounts of blue ink will generally have a great effect on white ink. (T or F)

When you order special inks, the manufacturer would probably ask you to supply the following:

_____ 7. Samples of the _____ to be printed on

_____ 8. The model of _____ you will use

_____ 9. The press operating _____

_____ 10. The _____ bar on the scale should be adjusted to zero to compensate for the weight of the glass or plastic plate on the scale platform.

_____ 11. An ink _____ test is performed by scraping a tiny dab of ink along the paper with the ink knife blade.

Match the ink characteristic with its correct description.

_____ 12. Measure of stickiness   a. Fugitive ink

_____ 13. An ink that tends to fade when exposed to sunlight   b. Length

_____ 14. Resistance to flow   c. Tack

_____ 15. Ability to be drawn out in long strings   d. Viscosity

Match the drying property with its correct description.

_____   16. The drying oils absorb oxygen from the air.   a. Evaporation

_____   17. Solvent and water on the sheet evaporate into the   b. Absorption
                          air.
_____   c. Oxidation
                     18. The solvent is absorbed into the paper.

_____   19. In printing with heat transfer inks on fabrics, the artwork is first printed
                          in the desired colors on paper. The printed sheet is contacted, with heat,
                          against the fabric. Finally, the _____ causes the ink to transfer to the
                          fabric.

Match each ink additive with its correct description.

_____   20. #0 varnish   a. Will improve the gloss and the drying of
                                                  printed inks
_____   21. Cobalt drier
                                              b. Will reduce an ink's tack without reducing its
_____   22. Tack reducer   body
                          (paste form)
                                              c. Too much may cause scumming and drying on
                                                  the rollers and in the fountain
_____   23. Tack reducer
                          (liquid)   d. Will reduce both an ink's tack and its body;
                                                  will also reduce linting
_____   24. Gloss paste

                                              e. Added to reduce the tack and body of light-
_____   25. Anti-oxidant spray   body inks; also improves the flow and transfer
                                                  of the ink

                                              f. Prevents ink from "skinning" overnight when
                                                  sprayed on the ink rollers and the fountain on
                                                  the press

Unit 15A
PAPERS AND PAPERCUTTING

(pages 239–246)   PHOTO-OFFSET FUNDAMENTALS

_____ 1. Mechanically ground wood _____ is produced by grinding logs into tiny particles.

_____ 2. New cotton pulp makes the finest grade of paper. (T or F)

The basic operations in papermaking are listed below. Letter them (a through f) in the order in which they take place.

_____ 3. Adding the sizing material

_____ 4. Coating the paper

_____ 5. Adding clay loader

_____ 6. Calendering the paper

_____ 7. Beating and refining the pulp

_____ 8. Forming the paper

_____ 9. The abbreviation *S&SC* means that the paper has been _____ and supercalendered.

Match each kind of paper with one of its common uses.

Kinds of Paper	Common Uses
10. Gummed paper	a. Business letterheads and office forms
11. Newsprint	b. Labels
12. Text offset	c. Newspapers, broadsides, and advertising circulars
13. Bond paper	d. Books, magazines, and catalogs

_____ 14. Undue pressure during press operation can cause _____ to appear on carbonless paper.

_____ 15. A #10 envelope is 4⅛ inches × _____.

_____ 16. A #6¾ envelope is _____ × 6½ inches.

_____ 17. A #88-B card is _____ × 3½ inches.

_____ 18. A #63 card is 2¼ inches × _____.

_____ 19. A #70 card is 2⅛ inches × _____.

_____ 20. You can avoid running a single small card on the offset press by ganging two, four, eight, or more to a single _____. They are cut apart afterwards.

_____ 21. The abbreviation for an envelope whose opening is on the narrow end is _____.

_____ 22. The abbreviation _____ indicates that the envelope flap is on the long side.

_____ 23. Thermal paper is sensitive to _____.

_____ 24. In the making of carbonless paper, the abbreviation for coated front and back is _____.

_____ 25. In the making of carbonless paper, the abbreviation for coating on back is _____.

_____ 26. Paper that has an adhesive on one side only, with peel-off backing, is called _____ paper.

_____ 27. Paper designated C1S should be stacked with the _____ side up.

_____ 28. Machine-finished paper is a relatively inexpensive paper to which a great deal of filler or sizing has been added. (T or F)

_____ 29. A ream of paper consists of _____ sheets.

Unit 15B
PAPERS AND PAPERCUTTING

(pages 246–259)   PHOTO-OFFSET FUNDAMENTALS

_____ 1. Print on the felt side of a sheet, rather than on the _____ side.

_____ 2. Cutter _____ may be picked up by the offset press blanket and cause hickies.

_____ 3. To determine the caliper of a sheet, measure the combined thickness of four sheets of that paper and divide by _____.

_____ 4. The number of leaves in a book with 348 pages is _____.

_____ 5. The number of paper thicknesses in a book with 348 pages is _____.

_____ 6. The thickness of three-ply paperboard (in thousandths of an inch) is generally _____.

_____ 7. Paper grain in a sheet may be either grain long or grain _____.

_____ 8. Generally, a sheet of paper will make a cleaner fold across the grain. (T or F)

_____ 9. The basic size of offset book paper (in inches) is _____.

_____ 10. The term *basis* means the same as _____.

_____ 11. Basis is the weight in pounds of _____ sheets of a basic size of a particular kind of paper.

_____ 12. A wrapped package of bond paper labeled "11 × 17–10 20-lb. Sub." weighs _____ pounds.

Refer to Figure 15-A. Answer the following questions concerning the label shown there:

Fig. 15-A

_____ 13. The number of sheets in the package is _____.

_____ 14. The grammage of the paper is _____.

_____ 15. The substance of this paper (in pounds) is _____.

_____ 16. The underlined dimension means that, for this paper, the _____ runs lengthwise.

_____ 17. The width (in millimeters) of this paper is _____.

_____ 18. The width, in inches, of this paper is _____.

_____ 19. In pounds, 1000 sheets of this paper would weigh _____.

_____ 20. The color of this paper is _____.

_____ 21. The number of these similarly wrapped packages you would need for 5000 sheets is _____.

_____ 22. The length of this paper in millimeters is _____.

_____ 23. If cut into 5½-inch × 8½-inch pieces, the paper would have a grain that runs short. (T or F)

_____ 24. How many 500-sheet reams of 17 × 22–20 bond are required to obtain 20,000 pieces 8½ inches × 11 inches?

_____ 25. How many pounds of 17 × 22–16 bond will yield 180,000 pieces 5½ inches × 8½ inches?

_____ 26. When the air measures 60% relative humidity, it contains _____% of the total amount of moisture it could hold.

_____ 27. Paper will usually tear more evenly and cleanly parallel with the direction of grain. (T or F)

_____ 28. Paper dampened on one side will usually roll up with the direction of the grain at a right angle to the axis of the roll. (T or F)

_____ 29. The abbreviation for grams per square meter is written as _____.

_____ 30. The unit of measure used to state metric sheet dimensions is the _____.

_____ 31. To convert inches to millimeters, multiply the number of inches by _____.

_____ 32. When converting paper sizes from inches to millimeters, round off any decimal fraction to the nearest whole _____.

_____ 33. Converted to metric, 5 inches × 8½ inches is _____.

_____ 34. To convert pounds to kilograms, multiply the weight in pounds by _____.

_____ 35. Two reams of 17 × 22–20 bond paper weigh _____ kilograms.

_____ 36. One pound of paper weighs _____ kilograms.

_____ 37. One pound of paper contains more sheets than one kilogram of paper. (T or F)

Give the basic sizes of the following kinds of paper (in inches):

_____ 38. Bond

_____ 39. Book

_____ 40. Cover

_____ 41. Onionskin

Refer to Figure 16-B, which is a schematic cross-section of a duplicator-size offset press. Identify the lettered parts.

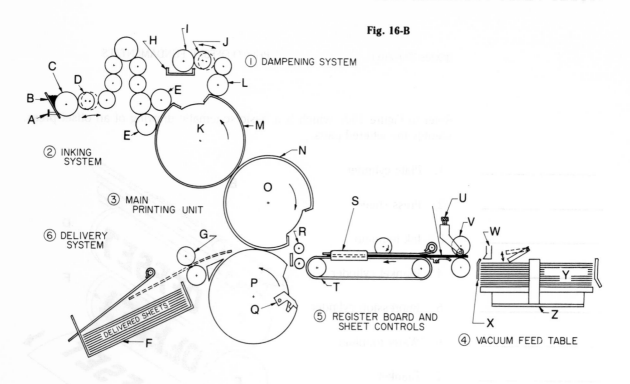

Fig. 16-B

15. Paper table

16. Ink ductor roller

17. Ink fountain roller

18. Paper pile

19. Double-sheet detector (sheet caliper)

20. Plate cylinder

21. Ink form roller

22. Gripper

23. Ejector wheels

24. Blanket cylinder

25. Ink fountain key (screw)

26. Impression cylinder

27. Water fountain

28. Ink fountain blade

_____ 29. Plate

_____ 30. Blanket

_____ 31. Water fountain roller

_____ 32. Delivery tray

_____ 33. Water ductor roller

_____ 34. Left side guide (jogger)

_____ 35. Pull-out rolls

_____ 36. Feed (forwarding) rolls

_____ 37. Dampener (water) form roller

_____ 38. Suction (sucker) foot

_____ 39. Conveyor tape

_____ 40. Sheet separators

Unit 16B
OFFSET PRESS FUNDAMENTALS

(pages 261–267)   PHOTO-OFFSET FUNDAMENTALS

_____ 1. The function of the dampening system is to supply a film of fountain solution to the surface of the offset _____.

Refer to Figure 16-C, which shows a conventional dampening system. Identify each of the lettered parts.

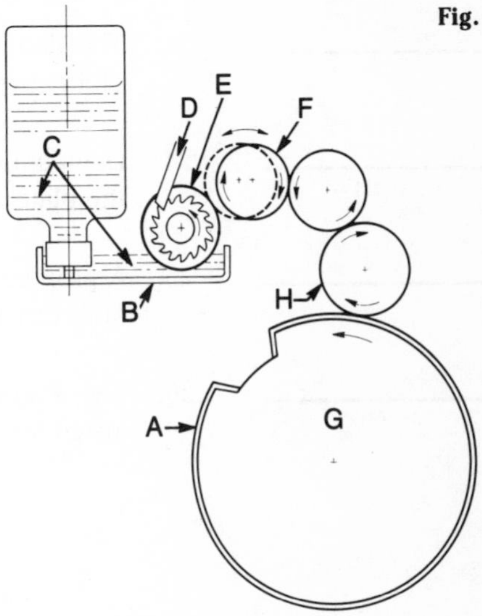

_____ 2. Fountain roller

_____ 3. Offset plate

_____ 4. Fountain

_____ 5. Ductor roller

_____ 6. Form roller

_____ 7. Plate cylinder

_____ 8. Fountain solution and bottle

_____ 9. Pawl

Fig. 16-C

_____ 10. Usually, as shown in Figure 16-C, the dampener form roller is driven by contact with the _____.

_____ 11. During normal operation of the press, the dampener fountain roller is always partially submerged in the fountain solution. (T or F)

_____ 12. The _____ roller transfers fountain solution from the fountain roller to the other dampener rollers.

_____ 13. Parallel adjustment of the Dahlgren and MiehleMatic metering roller results in uniform variation of solution all along the plate. (T or F)

_____ 14. Skewing the Dahlgren and MiehleMatic metering roller causes an increase in pressure at the _____, providing the end pressures are equal.

_____ 15. The Didde-Glaser dampening system emits directed _____ of fountain solution to the dampening rollers.

_____ 16. Sometimes a quantity of _____ arabic is added to the fountain solution to act as a mild etch.

_____ 17. The term *pH* means the degree of _____ or acidity of a solution.

18. If the fountain solution pH is too high, the plate may scum in the clear area. (T or F)

_____

19. The addition of alcohol to the fountain solution is not to exceed _____% by volume.

_____

20. Adding alcohol to the fountain solution speeds the _____ of moisture from the plate.

_____

21. To add large amounts of water quickly, turn the _____ roller knob by hand.

_____

22. A ratchet-control lever provides the desired speed of _____ of the fountain roller.

_____

23. The dampener form rollers on many presses may be provided with a cloth cover called a _____.

_____

24. Dampener form rollers should be able to prevent scum from reaching the plate and press _____.

_____

25. A properly adjusted dampener form roller should yield a slight drag on both test strips between roller and plate. (T or F)

_____

26. The amount of water allowed on certain areas of the plate can be adjusted by the use of water _____ added to the fountain system.

Unit 16C
OFFSET PRESS FUNDAMENTALS

(pages 267–270)   PHOTO-OFFSET FUNDAMENTALS

_____   1. The function of the inking system is to provide the proper amount of ink
                       to the offset _____ during the press run.

                   Refer to Figure 16-D, which shows a conventional inking system. Identify each
                   of the lettered parts.

Fig. 16-D

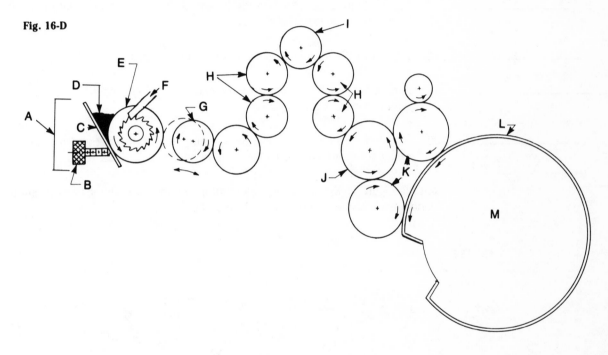

_____   2. Fountain blade

_____   3. Ink fountain assembly

_____   4. Fountain roller

_____   5. Ink key (adjusting screw)

_____   6. Plate cylinder

_____   7. Ink

_____   8. Form roller

_____   9. Pawl

_____   10. Offset plate

_____ 11. Oscillating roller

_____ 12. Ductor roller

_____ 13. Distribution roller

_____ 14. Idler rollers

_____ 15. In the inking system shown in Figure 16-D, the ink fountain roller is in constant contact with the ductor roller. (T or F)

_____ 16. The function of each ink fountain _____ is to adjust the thickness of ink film that the fountain roller draws through in that area.

_____ 17. Ink fountain _____ reduce the length of the ink fountain when narrow sheets are being run on the press.

_____ 18. Ink form rollers must be set parallel to the plate. (T or F)

_____ 19. A good test of the ink form rollers should yield an inked line of _____ width all across the plate.

_____ 20. In the combined inking and dampening system, the ink and the dampening solutions are fed to the plate by the same _____ roller(s).

Refer to Figure 16-E, which shows a combined inking and dampening system. Identify each of the lettered parts shown there.

Fig. 16-E

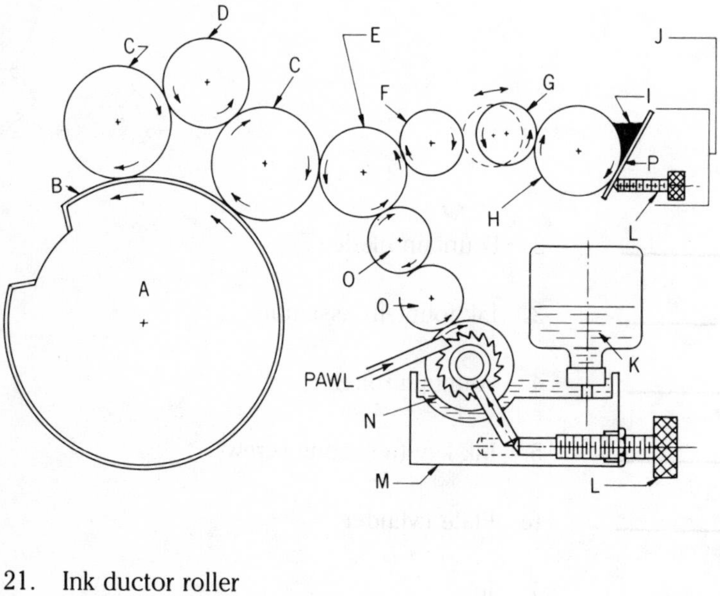

_____ 21. Ink ductor roller

_____ 22. Fountain solution

_____ 23. Plate cylinder

_____ 24. Adjusting screw (ink key)

_____ 25. Idler roller

_____ 26. Form roller

_____ 27. Water fountain

_____ 28. Ink fountain roller

_____ 29. Distribution rollers

_____ 30. Plate

_____ 31. Ink-and-water combining roller

_____ 32. Ink fountain assembly

_____ 33. Water fountain roller

_____ 34. Vibrator roller

_____ 35. Ink fountain blade

_____ 36. Ink

Class Name Date Score

Unit 16D

OFFSET PRESS FUNDAMENTALS

(pages 270–279) PHOTO-OFFSET FUNDAMENTALS

_______________ 1. In the main printing unit of an offset press, the _____ cylinder carries the offset plate.

_______________ 2. The inked plate image is transferred by the _____ which prints its image onto the paper sheet.

Refer to Figure 16-F, which shows a cross-section of a sheet-fed, single-color offset press. Identify the lettered parts.

_______________ 3. Impression cylinder

_______________ 4. Inking unit

_______________ 5. Plate

_______________ 6. Grippers

_______________ 7. Dampening unit

_______________ 8. Delivery cylinder

_______________ 9. Pile height guide

_______________ 10. Blanket

_______________ 11. Vacuum sucker foot

_______________ 12. Sheet being printed

_______________ 13. Feeder pile

_______________ 14. Blanket cylinder

_______________ 15. Plate cylinder

_______________ 16. Delivery pile

_______________ 17. Delivery-gripper chain

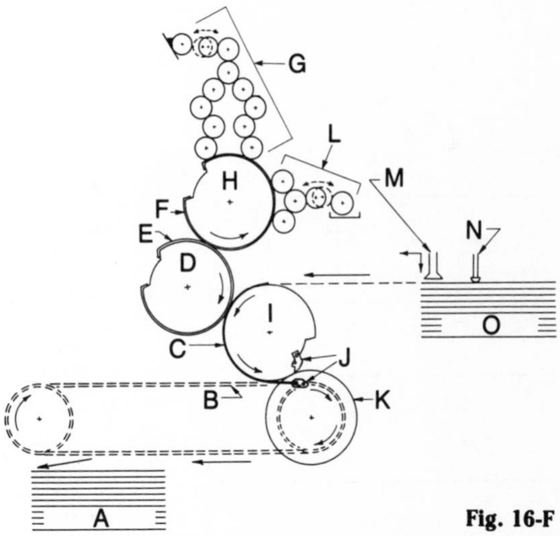

Fig. 16-F

18. The three-main-cylinder design of the offset press is similar to the four-main-cylinder design, but generally omits the _____ cylinder.

19. The two-main-cylinder design of press has the impression segment and the _____ segment as two halves of the same cylinder.

Refer to Figure 16-G. Answer the following questions.

Fig. 16-G

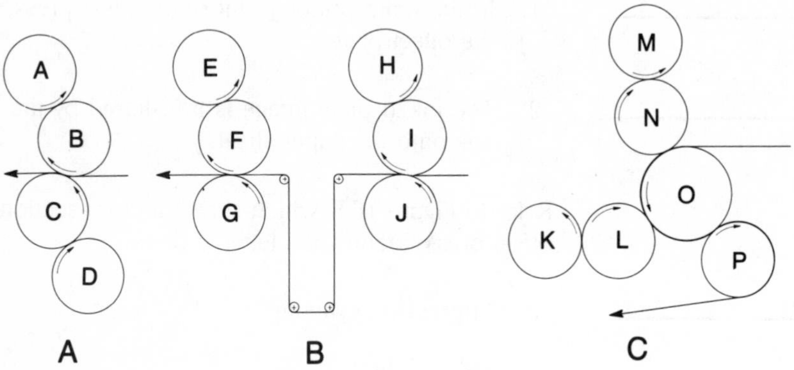

20. The press design _____ has one impression cylinder for the two printing couples.

21. The press shown in _____ is a perfecting press.

22. In the press shown in A, the _____ cylinders serve as impression cylinders for each other.

23. The number of colors that can be printed at one time in press design A is _____.

24. In press design C, parts L and N are _____ cylinders.

25. In press design C, the part lettered _____ is a delivery cylinder.

26. To adjust a plate for "skew," move both plate ends in the same direction. (T or F)

27. "Running down" a plate means to remove the excess _____ at the end of a press run.

28. A low spot in a blanket can be repaired by pasting one or more layers of _____ paper under the low spot.

Refer to Figure 16-H, which shows the installation of packing. Identify the lettered parts.

_____ 29. Bearer contact

_____ 30. Blanket cylinder

_____ 31. Blanket cylinder undercut

_____ 32. Plate cylinder

_____ 33. Plate cylinder undercut

_____ 34. Packing (under the plate)

_____ 35. Packing (under the blanket)

_____ 36. Blanket

_____ 37. Plate

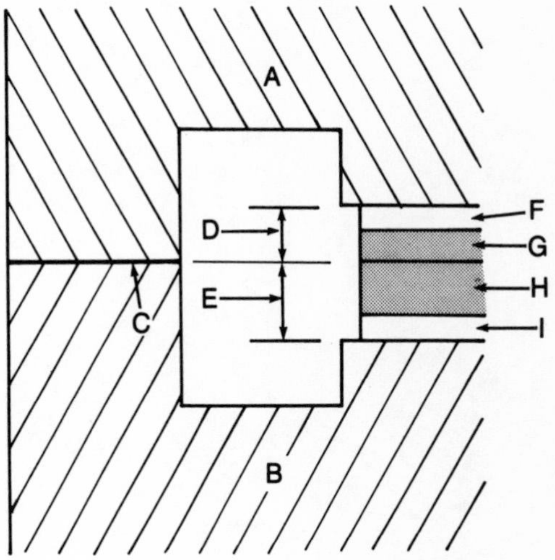

Fig. 16-H

_____ 38. The plate cylinder undercut provides for the thicknesses of the plate and the plate _____.

_____ 39. The bearers of the _____ cylinder are undercut below its body surface.

_____ 40. When the cylinders are properly packed, there will be no space between each pair of their opposing bearers. (T or F)

_____ 41. Undercut on the _____ cylinder allows the blanket cylinder to be adjusted toward or away from the impression cylinder.

_____ 42. The printed image can be lengthened a bit by transferring some packing from the _____ cylinder to the blanket cylinder.

Unit 16E
OFFSET PRESS FUNDAMENTALS

(pages 280–283)   PHOTO-OFFSET FUNDAMENTALS

_____ 1. Most press paper feeder units are air- and _____-operated.

Complete each of the following statements as they apply to the usual paper feeding-to-delivery system.

_____ 2. Sucker _____ pick up the top sheet in the paper pile.

_____ 3. Sheet _____ hold back all but the top sheet.

_____ 4. Sucker feet pass the sheet to the _____ rolls.

_____ 5. The conveyor tapes pass the sheet down the _____ table.

_____ 6. The front stop _____ stop the sheet.

_____ 7. The sheet is guided (jogged) across the table to a predetermined _____ position.

_____ 8. The sheet is propelled into the _____ cylinder grippers.

_____ 9. A slight buckling of the sheet ensures positive positioning at the _____.

_____ 10. The grippers carry the sheet between the _____ and the impression cylinders under pressure.

_____ 11. The paper is printed by the inked image on the _____ cylinder.

_____ 12. The printed sheet is ejected (or dropped) into a delivery _____.

_____ 13. If the press is equipped with a chain delivery system, the printed sheet is released into the stacker and is _____ automatically.

_____ 14. Undesirable offsetting of ink from the front of one sheet to the back of another is often called _____.

_____ 15. The chain delivery system has _____ bars mounted across endless chains.

_____ 16. In general, the chain delivery is a more positive delivery than simple ejector rolls. (T or F)

_____ 17. To prevent the smudging of freshly printed sheets, the stacker may be equipped with an anti-offset spray device. (T or F)

Refer to Figure 16-I, which shows part of the paper feeding-to-delivery system. Identify the lettered parts.

_____ 18. Gripper

_____ 19. Stop finger

_____ 20. Impression cylinder

_____ 21. Blanket

_____ 22. Sheet of paper

_____ 23. Blanket cylinder

_____ 24. Feed rollers

_____ 25. Conveyor tape

_____ 26. Buckle in sheet

Fig. 16-I

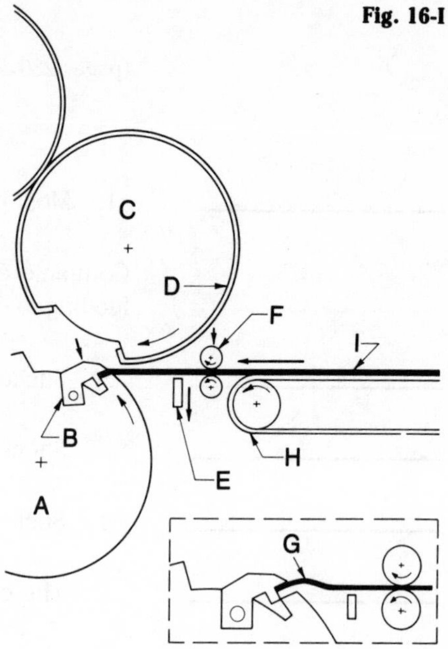

Unit 17A
OFFSET PRESS OPERATION

(pages 285–292)　　　　　　　PHOTO-OFFSET FUNDAMENTALS

_____ 1. When operating the press, you may need acetate or paper strips for use as _____ gauges.

_____ 2. Use the _____ to turn the press a revolution or two by hand to make sure the press will operate correctly.

Refer to Figure 17-A, which shows a Multilith 1360 vacuum blower pump. Identify the lettered parts.

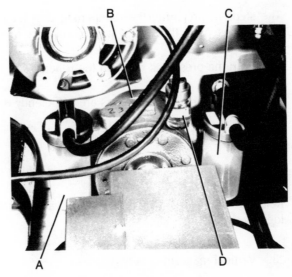

Fig. 17-A

_____ 3. Paper feeder pump

_____ 4. Oiler jar

_____ 5. Vacuum side air filter jar

_____ 6. Blower side air filter jar

_____ 7. To lubricate the press, use a nondetergent oil. (T or F)

The basic steps in preparing the inking unit for operation are listed below. Letter these steps (a through k) in the sequence in which they are performed.

_____ 8. Adjust fountain keys.

_____ 9. Adjust so ink ductor roller is out of contact with fountain roller.

117

_____ 10. Place ink in fountain.

_____ 11. Set ink fountain ratchet in usual running position.

_____ 12. Turn on press and allow it to ink up.

_____ 13. Set ink ductor roller ON.

_____ 14. Turn ink fountain ratchet to "full ON."

_____ 15. Turn night latch to OFF (rollers in contact).

_____ 16. Install ink fountain liner (if it is to be used).

_____ 17. Install ink fountain and rollers.

_____ 18. Shut off press.

The steps in preparing the dampening unit for operation are listed below. Letter the steps (a through d) in the sequence in which they are performed.

_____ 19. Start the press and dampen the rollers.

_____ 20. Stop the press when rollers are sufficiently damp.

_____ 21. Install the fountain and rollers.

_____ 22. Turn night latch to OFF (rollers in operating position).

Refer to Figure 17-B, which shows the vacuum feeder and paper magazine. Identify each of the lettered parts.

_____ 23. Vertical magazine guides

_____ 24. Sheet separator and brackets

_____ 25. Ruled scale

_____ 26. Pullout rolls

_____ 27. Blower tube

_____ 28. Suction foot

_____ 29. Multiple-sheet detector

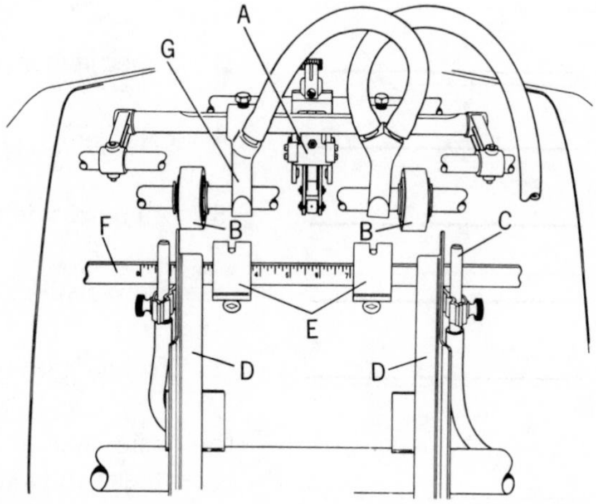

Fig. 17-B

Refer to Figure 17-C, which shows a conveyor board (register table). Identify each of the lettered component parts.

118

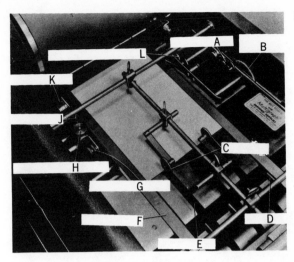

Fig. 17-C

_____ 30. Conveyor tape

_____ 31. Paper retainer

_____ 32. Stationary guide and clamp

_____ 33. Jogger guide micrometer adjustment

_____ 34. Micrometer lock

_____ 35. Jogger guide

_____ 36. Locating scale

_____ 37. Approximate adjustment

_____ 38. Parallel adjustment

_____ 39. Skid rolls

_____ 40. Tape guide

_____ 41. In preparing the offset press delivery for operation, set the jogger (stacker or delivery tray) for maximum _____.

_____ 42. Whenever you adjust for position of image, you generally must wash the old image from the _____.

_____ 43. A slight _____ adjustment of image can be made usually by moving the side guides.

_____ 44. A _____ image is one that is printed twisted (crooked) on the sheet.

_____ 45. A vertical adjustment moves the image up or down on the sheet. (T or F)

_____ 46. An _____ pressure that is too heavy will "squash out" the halftone dots.

Unit 17B
OFFSET PRESS OPERATION

(pages 292–299)   PHOTO-OFFSET FUNDAMENTALS

The main steps in the operation of the offset press are listed below. Letter the steps (a through e) in the sequence in which they are performed.

_____   1. Bring the plate into contact with the blanket.

_____   2. Feed the sheets.

_____   3. Drop the dampener form rollers.

_____   4. Turn on the press motor.

_____   5. Drop the ink form rollers.

The main steps in stopping the press are listed below. Letter these steps (a through e) in the sequence in which they are performed.

_____   6. Bring the plate out of contact with the blanket.

_____   7. Shut off the feeder.

_____   8. Lift the dampener form rollers.

_____   9. Turn off the press motor.

_____   10. Lift the ink form rollers.

_____   11. Three methods of washing the press are by hand, with a _____ sheet, and by using a roller-cleaning device.

_____   12. At least once a week, remove the _____ to rest it.

_____   13. Wipe down the blanket cylinder with a pad that has been moistened with _____.

Refer to Figure 17-D. Identify the three strip materials shown there.

_____   14. For creasing

_____   15. For perforating

_____   16. For slitting

Fig. 17-D

A

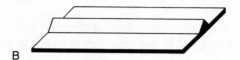

B

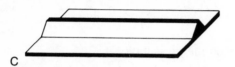

C

_____ 17. Strip materials may be attached directly to the _____ cylinder of the press to perform their function during the press run.

_____ 18. When using strip cutting materials against the blanket, use an old, spare _____ for these operations.

_____ 19. A factory-installed numbering unit may include one or more _____ heads.

_____ 20. A factory-installed numbering unit has its own _____ system.

_____ 21. In the machine thermography process, the excess _____ sprinkled on the sheet is vacuumed from the sheet.

_____ 22. An envelope usually varies from two to _____ thicknesses over its entire area.

_____ 23. Place the envelopes in the feeder with the _____ end to the front.

_____ 24. Adjust the impression for the _____ part of the envelope.

_____ 25. Adjust the double-sheet detector for the _____ part of the envelope.

_____ 26. Sometimes a weak area in part of the envelope's printed image may be corrected by building up that corresponding area on the impression cylinder with layers of cellophane tape. (T or F)

122

Refer to Figure 17-E, which shows one-half of an envelope. Indicate the number of thicknesses of paper in each of the lettered areas of the envelope.

27. A _____

28. B _____

29. C _____

30. D _____

31. E _____

32. F _____

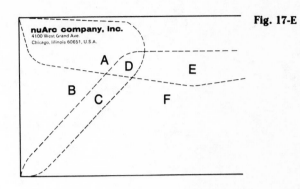

Fig. 17-E

nuArc company, Inc.
4100 West Grand Ave
Chicago, Illinois 60651, U.S.A.

A D E

B C F

Unit 18A
SHEET-FED PRESSES AND DUPLICATORS

(pages 300–308)   PHOTO-OFFSET FUNDAMENTALS

Refer to Figure 18-A, which shows a rotary press fitted with a roll converter. Identify the lettered parts.

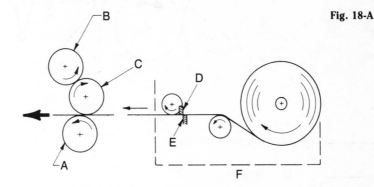

Fig. 18-A

_____   1.   Rotating knife

_____   2.   Roll converter

_____   3.   Blanket cylinder

_____   4.   Plate cylinder

_____   5.   Impression cylinder

_____   6.   Stationary knife

Refer to Figure 18-B, which shows a Multilith 1360. Identify each of the lettered parts.

_____   7.   Air blowers

_____   8.   Moisture form roller

_____   9.   Blanket cylinder

_____   10.   Skid wheels

_____   11.   Ink system

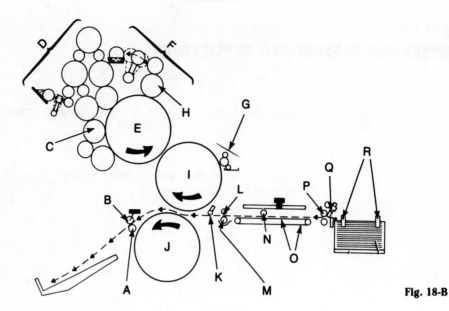

Fig. 18-B

_____   12. Ink form rollers

_____   13. Stop fingers

_____   14. Impression cylinder

_____   15. Paper-ejector wheels

_____   16. Paper-guide assembly

_____   17. Moisture system

_____   18. Optional blanket cleaner

_____   19. Vacuum feet

_____   20. Paper-ejector roller

_____   21. Pullout wheels

_____   22. Feed rollers

_____   23. Master cylinder

_____   24. Sheet transport tapes

Refer to Figure 18-C. Identify the various positions of the Multi 1360 single-lever control.

_____   25.   Dampener form roller ON

_____   26.   PRINT position

_____   27.   Ink and dampener form
                        roller ON

_____   28.   OFF position

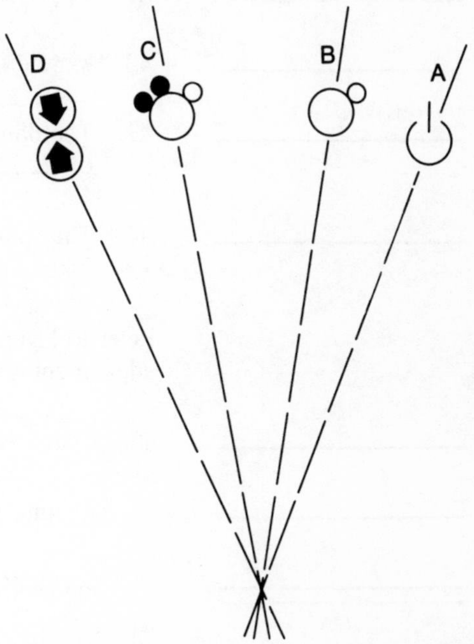

Fig. 18-C

The major steps in the operation of the Multi 1360 are listed below. Letter these steps (a through l) in the order in which they are performed.

_____   29.   Start the press (pushbutton K).

_____   30.   Actuate the sheet-feed control.

_____   31.   Moisten the plate.

_____   32.   Set the single-lever control to INK position.

_____   33.   Turn off the sheet-feed control.

_____   34.   Set the single-lever control to MOIST position.

_____   35.   Set the single-lever control to PRINT position.

_____   36.   Turn press off (K).

_____   37.   Move the single-lever control to OFF position.

_____   38.   Print the required number of copies.

_____   39.   Remove the plate.

_____   40.   Clean the blanket.

List the ink-form-roller-to-plate test ink stripe widths for the following rollers:

_____   41.   Upper form rollers

_____   42.   Middle form roller

_____   43.   The dampener-form-roller-to-plate pressure test is made with two strips of _____-pound paper or with strips of 75 g/m^2 paper.

_____   44.   The plate-cylinder-to-blanket-cylinder pressure test should produce inked lines on the blanket that measure ⅛ inch to _____ in width.

Refer to Figure 18-D, which shows the standard impression-cylinder pressure adjustment device. Identify the lettered parts.

_____   45.   Clamp screw

_____   46.   Alemite fitting

_____   47.   Segment

_____   48.   Adjusting screw

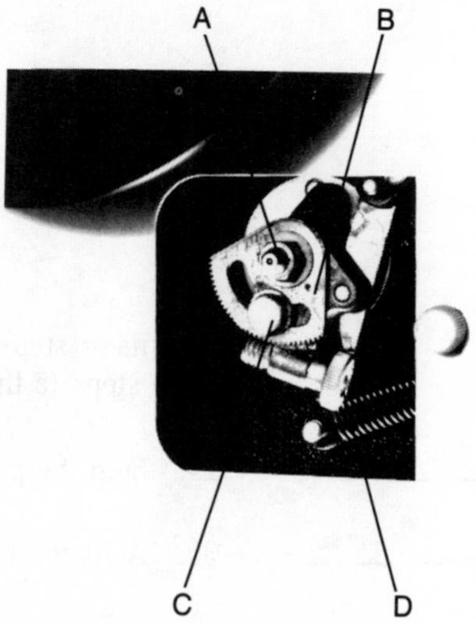

Fig. 18-D

128

Class Name Date Score

Unit 18B

SHEET-FED PRESSES AND DUPLICATORS

(pages 308–310) PHOTO-OFFSET FUNDAMENTALS

Refer to Figure 18-E, which shows the Heidelberg Model KORD. Identify the lettered parts.

______ 1. Plate cylinder

______ 2. Inking system

______ 3. Feed pile

______ 4. Dampening system

______ 5. Pre-loader

______ 6. Delivery chain

______ 7. Impression cylinder

______ 8. Blanket cylinder

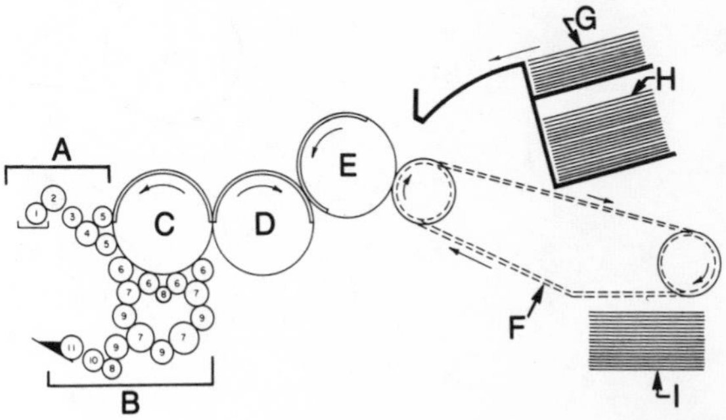

Fig. 18-E

Answer the following questions about the Heidelberg Model KORD:

______ 9. For letterset operation, the ______ system is not used.

______ 10. Feeding and ______ of paper are at the same end of the press.

______ 11. The press is designed and equipped for both letterset and ______ printing.

Refer to Figure 18-F, which shows the inking and dampening rollers on the ATF Chief 20 press. Identify the lettered rollers.

______ 12. Dampener form roller (upper)

______ 13. Ink form roller (right)

______ 14. Dampener form roller (lower)

______ 15. Ink form roller (left)

______ 16. Water fountain roller

______ 17. Ink fountain roller

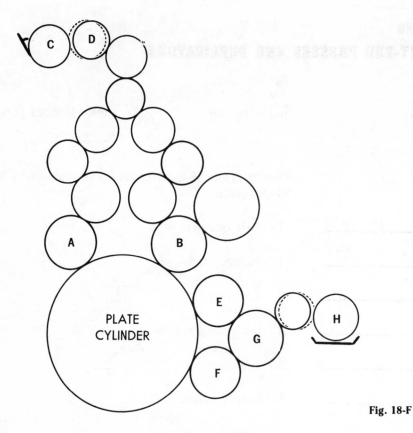

Fig. 18-F

_____ 18. Ink ductor roller

_____ 19. Vibrator roller

_____ 20. The ATF Chief 20A press prints in one color in one pass through the press. (T or F)

_____ 21. The ATF Chief 20A press has a maximum sheet size of 14 × _____ inches.

_____ 22. The ATF Chief 20A uses a _____ delivery.

Unit 18C
SHEET-FED PRESSES AND DUPLICATORS

(pages 311–320)   PHOTO-OFFSET FUNDAMENTALS

Refer to Figure 18-G, which shows the ATF-Davidson Super Chief. Identify the lettered parts.

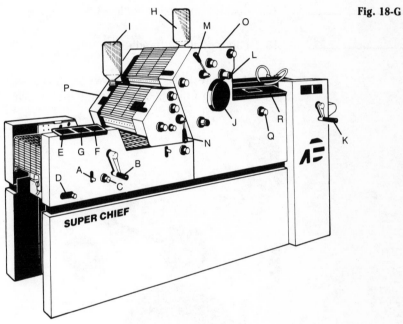

Fig. 18-G

_____   1.   Delivery pile handle

_____   2.   Delivery platform lowering rate adjustment

_____   3.   Second unit single-control lever

_____   4.   Second printing (color) unit

_____   5.   Delivery light switch

_____   6.   First unit single-control lever

_____   7.   Copy counter

_____   8.   Delivery lock release

_____   9.   Delivery end vacuum on–off control

_____   10. First unit image set knob

_____ 11. Control panel, feed end

_____ 12. Delivery panel machine stop switch

_____ 13. First printing (color) unit

_____ 14. Handwheel

_____ 15. Jogger (side guide) adjustment

_____ 16. First unit water bottle

_____ 17. Second unit water bottle

_____ 18. Paper platform handle

Refer to Figure 18-H, which shows the positions of the single-control lever on the ATF Super Chief 2000. Complete the following statements:

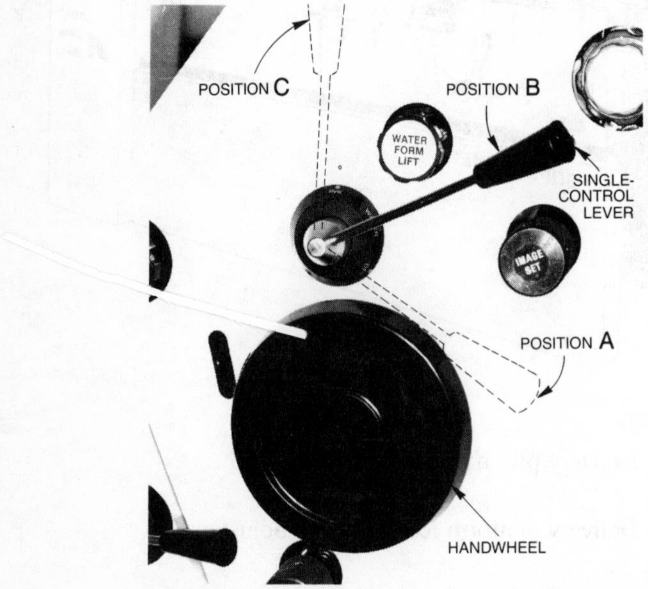

Fig. 18-H

_____ 19. In position A, water and ink form rollers are in the _____ position.

_____ 20. In position B, the water form roller contacts the _____; the ink form rollers are OFF.

_____ 21. In position _____, both water and ink form rollers are in contact with the plate.

_____ 22. The ATF Super Chief 2000 has two separate color-printing units. (T or F)

_____ 23. The main control panel for the ATF Super Chief 2000 is at the _____ end of the press.

132

_____ 24. An auxiliary press control panel is located at the _____ end of the press.

_____ 25. The maximum size of the sheet that this press series will accommodate is _____ × 17 inches.

_____ 26. With this sheet area capacity, the number of impressions required to print 10,000 8½-inch × 11-inch letterheads, one color, is _____. (Use the full capacity of the sheet.)

Refer to Figure 18-I, which shows a Vandercook flat-bed offset press. Identify the lettered parts of the press.

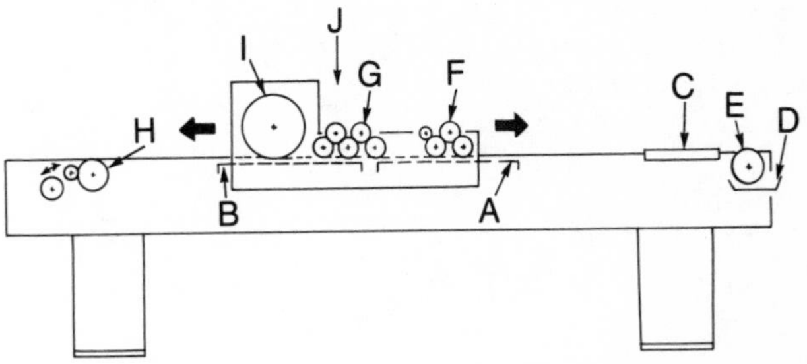

Fig. 18-I

_____ 27. Ink drum

_____ 28. Sheet bed

_____ 29. Ink rollers

_____ 30. Carriage

_____ 31. Blanket cylinder

_____ 32. Plate bed

_____ 33. Water drum

_____ 34. Dampening pad

_____ 35. Dampener rollers

_____ 36. Water tray

_____ 37. On the Vandercook press shown in Figure 18-I, the traveling (reciprocating) carriage carries the blanket cylinder and the _____ and dampening form rollers.

_____ 38. On the Vandercook press shown in Figure 18-I, the plate and the paper sheet are flat—not rolled—during the entire printing operation. (T or F)

Unit 19
THE WEB OFFSET PRESS

(pages 322–330)   PHOTO-OFFSET FUNDAMENTALS

Refer to Figure 19-A, which shows a four-unit, blanket-to-blanket web press. Identify each of the lettered components.

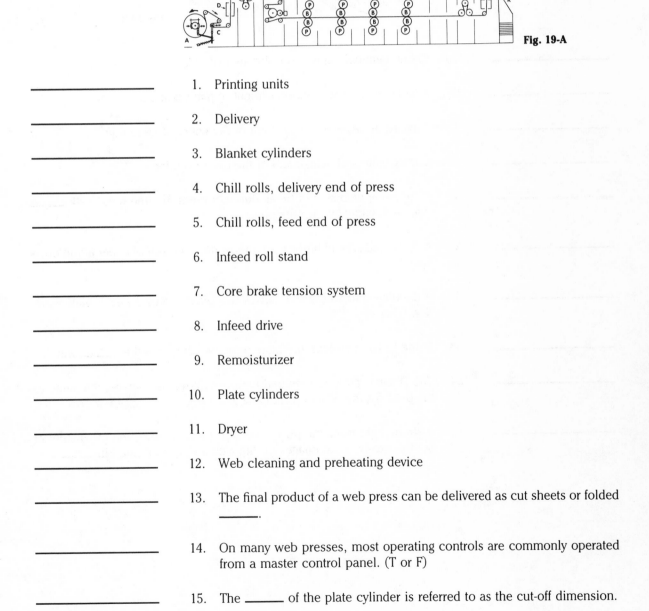

Fig. 19-A

1. Printing units

_____   2. Delivery

_____   3. Blanket cylinders

_____   4. Chill rolls, delivery end of press

_____   5. Chill rolls, feed end of press

_____   6. Infeed roll stand

_____   7. Core brake tension system

_____   8. Infeed drive

_____   9. Remoisturizer

_____   10. Plate cylinders

_____   11. Dryer

_____   12. Web cleaning and preheating device

_____   13. The final product of a web press can be delivered as cut sheets or folded _____.

_____   14. On many web presses, most operating controls are commonly operated from a master control panel. (T or F)

_____   15. The _____ of the plate cylinder is referred to as the cut-off dimension.

Refer to Figure 19-B, which shows the register adjustments on one web offset press model. Identify the lettered adjustments.

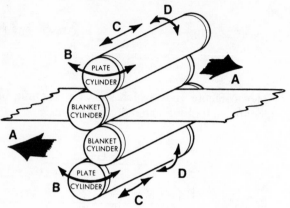

Fig. 19-B

_____ 16. Circumferential adjustment of plate cylinder

_____ 17. Angular (plate-cocking) adjustment of plate cylinder

_____ 18. Forward or backward movement of the entire printing unit

_____ 19. Lateral (side lay) adjustment of the plate cylinder

_____ 20. If the paper web should break during a press run, the web-break _____ will automatically stop the press.

_____ 21. A flying _____ will replace an almost depleted roll of paper at full press speed.

_____ 22. A double-ender web press carries two offset plates on each plate cylinder. (T or F)

_____ 23. In the Di-Litho system, the plate prints directly onto the _____ web.

_____ 24. The Di-Litho plate is prepared with a right-reading image, the same as the plate for the offset press. (T or F)

_____ 25. A strobe light gives the press operator a visual indication of whether or not the two or more images on the web are being printed in _____.

Unit 20

OFFSET PRESS TROUBLESHOOTING

(pages 331–339)   PHOTO-OFFSET FUNDAMENTALS

Name each of the problems described in the following statements:

1. The plate picks up ink in the clear areas and transfers it to the sheet.

2. There is uniform, light-colored tint over the entire sheet.

3. The type matter and the halftones fill up with ink on the printed sheet and plate.

4. Black spots appear in the blank areas of the printed image, and white spots appear in the solid (printed) areas.

5. The sheets stick together in the stacker (receiver) or delivery pile. The sheets tear when pulled apart.

6. The ink is penetrating the paper stock. The ink can be seen on the reverse side of the sheet.

7. The printed type is gray instead of black (when black ink is used).

8. The ink may spray over the press, especially at high temperatures.

9. There is a muddy image on the paper. The ink does not cover evenly.

10. The ink builds up, or piles up, on either the blanket or the plate, or both.

11. There is a gradual disappearance of some lines and halftone dots from the plate image.

12. The reverse side of the sheet is picking up an image from the printed sheet below it in the stacker.

13. Image is unevenly printed, probably caused by bare sections on the roller surface.

Identify the probable cause of each of the conditions listed below.

	Conditions	**Probable Cause**
_____	14. Blurred image on paper	a. Cocked plate
_____	15. Image not square on the sheet	b. Loose blanket
_____	16. White spot in halftone shadow area	c. Loose feeder side
_____	17. Out of register	d. Hicky

_____ 18. A hicky is a particle of foreign matter that attaches itself to the offset _____ or blanket.

_____ 19. On the printed sheet, the hicky appears as a black or _____ spot.

_____ 20. One way to prevent hickies is to use an ink knife to agitate the _____ in the fountain at intervals.

_____ 21. To prevent injury to your hands and the press, always stop the press before manually attempting to remove any hicky or other foreign particle from the press. (T or F)

Class Name Date Score

Unit 21

BINDERY (FINISHING) OPERATIONS

(pages 342–359) PHOTO-OFFSET FUNDAMENTALS

_______________ 1. The punching of rows of very tiny holes between postage stamps is an example of ______.

_______________ 2. ______ produces a raised ridge across a sheet so it will fold more easily.

Refer to Figure 21-A, which shows a simple setup for bench-top padding. Identify each of the lettered items shown.

_______________ 3. Top board

_______________ 4. Pad sheets

_______________ 5. Weight

_______________ 6. Bottom board

_______________ 7. Cemented surface of pads

_______________ 8. Chipboard

_______________ 9. Bench top

_______________ 10. Protective sheet of paper

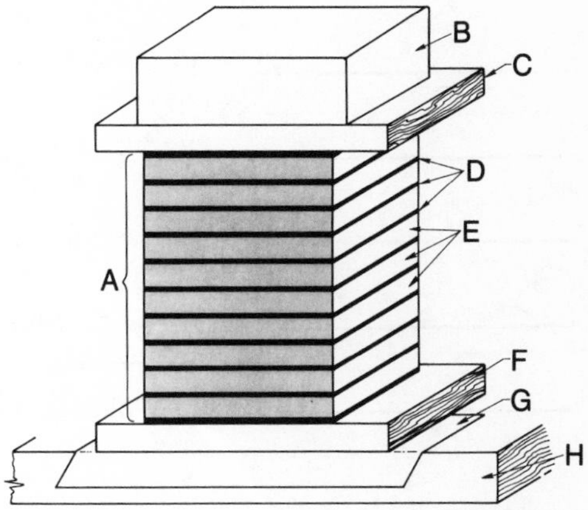

Fig. 21-A

The six basic steps in perfect binding are listed below. Letter these steps (a through f) in the order in which they are performed.

_______________ 11. Cut off the folded edge(s).

_______________ 12. Rough up the spine.

_______________ 13. Apply adhesive over the super.

_______________ 14. Apply super (gauze).

_______________ 15. Apply the cover(s).

_______________ 16. Apply adhesive to the spine.

Refer to Figure 21-B. Identify, by letter, the common paper folds shown there.

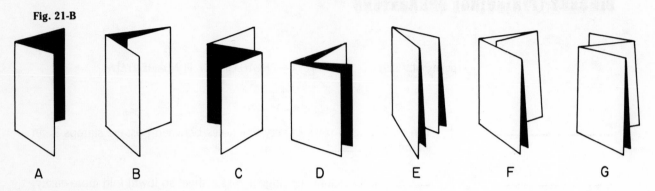

Fig. 21-B

A   B   C   D   E   F   G

_____ 17. Eight-page parallel fold

_____ 18. Eight-page right-angle (French fold) booklet

_____ 19. Twelve-page accordion, plus right-angle fold

_____ 20. Twelve-page baronial fold

_____ 21. Single fold; four-page leaflet

_____ 22. Accordion fold

_____ 23. Standard (double) fold

_____ 24. The terms _____ and collating are often used interchangeably.

_____ 25. The placing and fastening of a single page between the folded signatures of a book is an example of _____.

Unit 22

LEGAL RESTRICTIONS ON COPYING

(pages 360–364)   PHOTO-OFFSET FUNDAMENTALS

1. Information on copyrights and copyright procedures is available from the Copyright Office, Library of _____, Washington, DC.

2. A copyright is a form of legal _____ given to authors of literary and similar works.

3. The _____ owner has the exclusive right to copy, sell, and distribute that work.

4. The copyright notice should contain the word *Copyright,* the abbreviation *Copr.,* or the symbol _____.

5. The copyright notice should also consist of the name of the copyright _____ and the year of publication.

In the blanks, indicate by *yes* or *no* whether each of the following items can be copyrighted:

6. Calendar

7. Tape measure

8. Book

9. Schedule of sporting events

10. Labels

11. Musical compositions

12. Photographs

13. Maps

14. Catalogs

15. Listing of ingredients

16. Under the new law, works copyrighted before 1978, and in their first term of copyright, are protected for _____ years.

17. A work created after January 1, 1978, is automatically protected from the moment of its creation for the author's lifetime, plus _____ years after his or her death.

_____ 18. If you are not sure that a work is copyrighted, write the _____ for permission to reproduce.

_____ 19. Work that is copied with permission should carry a courtesy or credit line to indicate its source. (T or F)

_____ 20. Photographs that show clearly recognizable faces of persons cannot be used for advertising purposes without first obtaining written consent of the persons involved. (T or F)

_____ 21. If you are requested to reproduce obligations, securities, or paper money of the United States or other countries, report this at once to the Department of the _____, United States Secret Service, Washington, DC.

In the blanks, indicate by *yes* or *no* whether you may legally reproduce one or more copies of the following:

_____ 22. An automobile driver's license

_____ 23. Your birth certificate

_____ 24. Your school report card

_____ 25. An armed forces identification card

_____ 26. An amateur radio operator's license

_____ 27. A last will and testament

_____ 28. Illustrations from a copyrighted book

Unit 23

APPENDIX: INSTRUCTIONS FOR USING
THE KODAK HALFTONE CALCULATOR Q-15

(pages 365–382)   PHOTO-OFFSET FUNDAMENTALS

1. A contact screen is used when exposing for the main-exposure test negative (Steps 1 through 5). (T or F)

2. When exposing for the main-exposure test negative (Steps 1 through 5), the number of exposures made is _____.

3. When exposing for the no-screen bump exposure (Steps 6 through 8), the number of exposures made is _____.

4. When exposing for the no-screen bump exposure (Steps 6 through 8), no halftone screen is used. (T or F)

5. When exposing for the flash-exposure test negative (Steps 9 through 16), the number of sheets of film used is _____.

6. When exposing for the flash-exposure test negative (Steps 9 through 16), a halftone screen is used. (T or F)

7. As in Step 18, from each of the two halftone negatives of the gray scale, select a printable _____ dot, and a printable shadow dot.

8. As in Step 18, from the flash-exposure test negative, select a printable _____ dot.

9. Record your test results (as in Step 19) by showing the densities of the test negatives and the lengths of the _____ required.

Questions 10 through 16 refer to setting (calibrating) the calculator (Steps 20 through 25).

10. Set Ⓐ at the density of the _____ dot from Step 19a.

11. Set Tab _____ so that the length of the main exposure from Step 19e is indicated in the window at Ⓐ.

12. Rotate Ⓒ to the density of the _____ dot from Step 19b.

13. Rotate the clear dial (basic flash dial) until the _____ exposure time determined in Step 19d is centered in the slot.

14. Tape all three _____ together.

_____ 15. Tape Tab _____ to the yellow base.

_____ 16. On the _____ dial, locate the density of the highlight dot from Step 19c. Make a mark on the red dial opposite that density. Label the mark 10%.

Questions 17 through 22 refer to the use of the calibrated calculator for basic production procedures (Steps 26 through 30).

_____ 17. Determine the highlight and shadow _____ of your copy.

_____ 18. Place your copy on the camera _____.

_____ 19. Set Ⓐ at the _____ density of the copy.

_____ 20. Set Ⓓ at the _____ density of the copy.

_____ 21. Read the _____ exposure in the window at Ⓐ.

_____ 22. The required _____ exposure is indicated behind the hairline of Ⓓ.